THIS BOOK BELONGS TO

START DATE

SHE READS TRUTH

SUBSCRIPTION INQUIRIES
orders@shereadstruth.com

SHE READS TRUTH™

ISBN 978-1-962221-48-1

1 2 3 4 5 6 7 8 9 10

Though the dates, locations, and individuals in this book have been carefully researched, scholars disagree on many of these topics.

Research support provided by Logos Bible Software™. Learn more at logos.com.

@SHEREADSTRUTH

Download the She Reads Truth app, available for iOS and Android

Subscribe to the She Reads Truth Podcast

SHEREADSTRUTH.COM

This book was printed offset in Nashville, Tennessee, on 70# Lynx Opaque. Cover is 100# Cougar Opaque with a soft touch lamination.

BLESS THE LORD

READING THE PSALMS FOR LENT

SHE READS TRUTH

THE PSALMS ARE EVIDENCE *of a* GOD WHO INVITES US *to* BRING OUR WHOLE SELVES *to* HIM.

Amanda
Amanda Bible Williams
CO-FOUNDER

D*isgrace. Affliction. Worthless idols. Faithful love.*
Distress and grief.
Refuge and trust.

The words of Psalm 31 seemed to come to life on the page as I sat at the dining room table, Bible open and coffee in hand. I was not feeling disgraced or afflicted at the moment, not in distress or grieving anything in particular. It had been a good start to an ordinary day. But the honesty and intimacy of the prayer captivated me. I jotted down a paraphrase in the margin: "When I feel unseen and alone, He is still there, still listening for my cry."

Fast forward three hours, and the scene had shifted. It was a storyline I did not see coming, and boy did it sting. I felt blindsided and betrayed, and yes, even disgraced. My husband was there when the wave hit, and he held me as my shoulders shook with sobs. "It hurts," I said, as much to God as to him. "I don't understand."

And the Lord heard my cry.

It's incredible, isn't it? God's love for us is so deep, so secure, so present with us that He hears our groans and collects our tears (Ps 31:22; 56:8). He sees our affliction and knows the troubles of our souls (Ps 31:7). Yet somehow we convince ourselves that God wants only the tidiest version of us. We assume that only our prettiest prayers are welcome in His presence. Praise God, that isn't true!

The psalms are evidence of a God who invites us to bring our whole selves to Him. These poems and prayers demonstrate the radical closeness we have with God—in every emotion and circumstance, today and every day—through the cross of Jesus Christ. Access, intimacy, and irrevocable belonging are ours because our God pursued us with His presence all the way to death and back. Underneath every expression of praise, adoration, petition, and lament in the psalms lays an unshakeable foundation: the character of our good God proven in the life, death, and resurrection of Jesus.

I feel needy for the psalms in this season. Lent is a time of remembering and repenting, reorienting our hearts to the truth of who God is and who we are in Him. It requires honesty, patience, and the pain of a heart broken for the reality of sin and suffering. As we read the book of Psalms for Lent, I pray we will respond to the invitation to bare our hearts before God as His beloved children. May this ancient prayerbook teach us to question and yet trust, grieve and yet worship. Let's savor the psalms as they lead us day by day, verse by verse, into Holy Week. There we will witness again the act of radical love and power that has rescued our hearts and reconciled us to God forever.

Bless the Lord, O my soul!

DESIGN *on* PURPOSE

At She Reads Truth, we believe in pairing the inherently beautiful Word of God with the aesthetic beauty it deserves. Each of our resources is thoughtfully and artfully designed to highlight the beauty, goodness, and truth of Scripture in a way that reflects the themes of each curated reading plan.

The book of Psalms offers us authentic ways to continually express lament, repentance, and hardship to God with reverence and hope. The botanical imagery, layouts, and font choices in this book all contribute to these themes and have been curated to help you move through the season of Lent with worship as your guide.

Alongside photographs of florals, we created botanical bas-reliefs—a preservation method that uses air-dry clay and plaster to create artwork imprinted with floral designs—to symbolize the enduring message of the book of Psalms. They serve as a reminder of the way God has preserved these experiences of faithful psalmists so that we can now garner wisdom and encouragement from them.

The pairing of an elegant script and simple serif font highlight how the accessibility of the psalms help us to approach God with vulnerability, honesty, and authenticity. Some of the text in this book is formatted in a spiral pattern, an ode to the cyclical nature of the Psalms—they are well worn paths that we can come back to as needed to reconnect with God through the timeless words of the psalms. As you read, may you ever turn back to the hope we have in Christ.

HOW TO USE THIS BOOK

She Reads Truth is a community of women dedicated to reading the Word of God every day. In this **Bless the Lord: Reading the Psalms for Lent** reading plan, we will read the book of Psalms to praise God for who He is and His redemption. We will also read from the Last Supper to Resurrection Sunday to connect our time in the book of psalms to Jesus's saving work.

READ & REFLECT

Your **Bless the Lord: Reading the Psalms for Lent** book focuses primarily on Scripture, with added features to come alongside your time with God's Word.

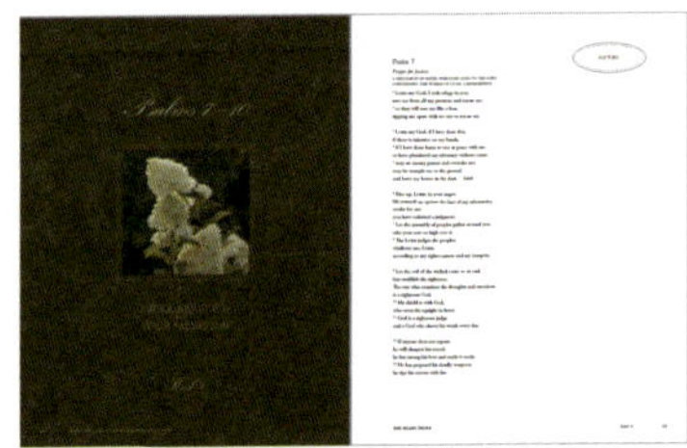

SCRIPTURE READING

Designed for a Monday start, this seven-week reading plan presents the book of Psalms in daily readings. The last four reading days focus on the final events of Holy Week.

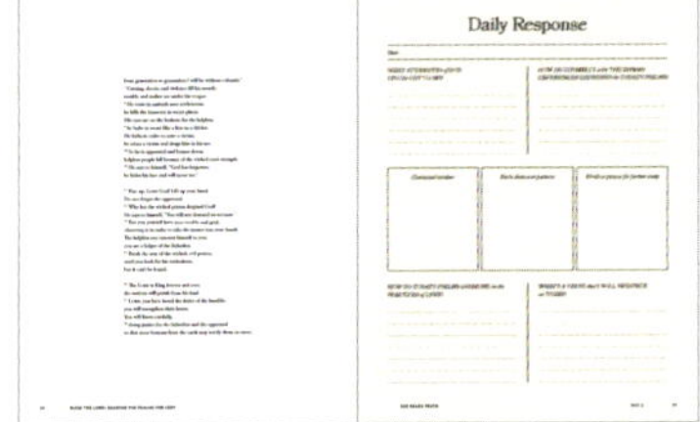

REFLECTION AND RESPONSE

Each weekday features an interactive worksheet to reflect on your reading, and a weekly prayer prompt will guide you in how to incorporate the psalms into your time of prayer.

COMMUNITY & CONVERSATION

You can start reading this book at any time! If you want to join women from Green Bay to Germany as they read along with you, join us in the **Lent 2026: Bless the Lord** reading plan through our app or website and podcast.

SHE READS TRUTH APP

Devotionals corresponding to each daily reading can be found in the **Lent 2026: Bless the Lord** reading plan in the She Reads Truth app. You can use the app to participate in community discussion and more.

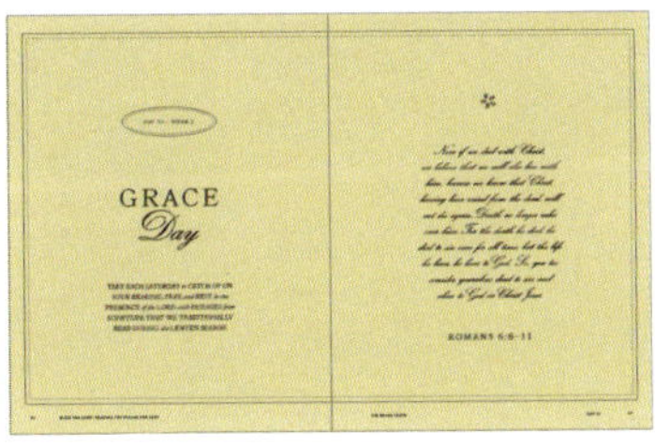

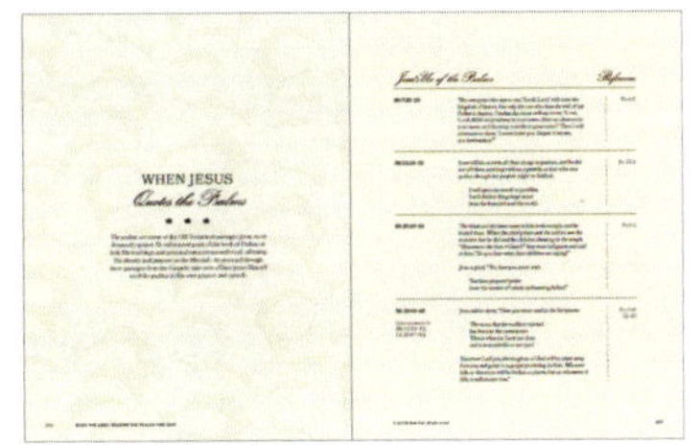

GRACE DAY

Use Saturdays to catch up on your reading, pray, and rest in the presence of the Lord.

WEEKLY TRUTH

Sundays offer the Hallel psalms to close the week (you'll read more about Hallel psalms on page 52) and are also set aside for Scripture memorization.

See tips for memorizing Scripture on page 272.

EXTRAS

This book features additional tools to help you gain a deeper understanding of the text.

Find a complete list of extras on page 13.

SHEREADSTRUTH.COM

The **Lent 2026: Bless the Lord** reading plan and devotionals will also be available at SheReadsTruth.com as the community reads each day. Invite your family, friends, and neighbors to read along with you!

SHE READS TRUTH PODCAST

Subscribe to the She Reads Truth Podcast, and join our founders and their guests each week as they talk about what you'll read in the week ahead.

Tune into episodes 317–323 for our **Lent 2026: Bless the Lord** series.

TABLE *of* CONTENTS

Week 1

DAY 1 Psalms 1–6 20
DAY 2 Psalms 7–10 24
DAY 3 Psalms 11–16 30
DAY 4 Psalms 17–18 35
DAY 5 Psalms 19–22 41
EXAMPLE RESPONSE 46
WEEK ONE RESPONSE 48
DAY 6 Grace Day 50
DAY 7 Weekly Truth 52

Week 2

DAY 8 Psalms 23–29 54
DAY 9 Psalms 30–34 62
DAY 10 Psalms 35–37 68
DAY 11 Psalms 38–41 75
DAY 12 Psalms 42–45 80
WEEK TWO RESPONSE 84
DAY 13 Grace Day 86
DAY 14 Weekly Truth 88

Week 3

DAY 15 Psalms 46–49 90
DAY 16 Psalms 50–54 97
DAY 17 Psalms 55–58 102
DAY 18 Psalms 59–64 107
DAY 19 Psalms 65–68 112
WEEK THREE RESPONSE 118
DAY 20 Grace Day 120
DAY 21 Weekly Truth 122

TABLE *of* CONTENTS

Week 4

DAY 22 Psalms 69–72 124
DAY 23 Psalms 73–76 131
DAY 24 Psalms 77–79 136
DAY 25 Psalms 80–85 147
DAY 26 Psalms 86–89 152
WEEK FOUR RESPONSE 158
DAY 27 Grace Day 160
DAY 28 Weekly Truth 162

Week 5

DAY 29 Psalms 90–95 164
DAY 30 Psalms 96–102 170
DAY 31 Psalms 103–105 176
DAY 32 Psalms 106–107 184
DAY 33 Psalms 108–112 189
WEEK FIVE RESPONSE 194
DAY 34 Grace Day 196
DAY 35 Weekly Truth 198

Week 6

DAY 36 Psalm 119:1–88 200
DAY 37 Psalm 119:89–176 206
DAY 38 Psalms 120–127 212
DAY 39 Psalms 128–134 216
DAY 40 Psalms 135–139 221
WEEK SIX RESPONSE 226
DAY 41 Grace Day 228
DAY 42 Weekly Truth 230

Week 7

DAY 43	Psalms 140–143	232
DAY 44	Psalms 144–146	241
DAY 45	Psalms 147–150	244
DAY 46	The Last Supper	250
DAY 47	Good Friday	254
WEEK SEVEN RESPONSE		258
DAY 48	Holy Saturday	260
DAY 49	Easter Sunday	262

Extras

She Reads Psalms	14
Tips for Reading Psalms	18
Activity: Floral Clay Molds	60
Hymn: What Wondrous Love Is This	94
"I Will" Statements in the Psalms	143
Hymn: Praise to the Lord, the Almighty	182
When Jesus Quotes the Psalms	236
Holy Week	248
A Glossary of Terms for Reading Psalms	268
For the Record	275

Key Verse

LET ALL WHO SEEK YOU
REJOICE AND BE GLAD IN YOU;
LET THOSE WHO LOVE YOUR
SALVATION CONTINUALLY SAY,
"THE LORD IS GREAT!"

PSALM 40:16

She Reads PSALMS

TIME TO READ PSALMS: 4 HOURS, 51 MINUTES

ON THE TIMELINE

The book of Psalms consists of many different hymns, songs, and prayers composed for faithful, heartfelt communication with God. The date of their composition ranges from the time of Moses (fifteenth century BC) to a time following the exile (sixth century BC or later). The different psalms were collected and arranged by editors after the Babylonian exile.

A LITTLE BACKGROUND

The Psalter (another name for the book of Psalms) is one large book made up of five smaller books, each arranged to thematically tell the story of Israel's history within the context of God's eternal kingdom. While some of the individual psalm headings contain historical information that might indicate the setting or author of a particular psalm, this is subject to interpretation. The most common designation in these subtitles is "of David," which likely refers to King David. David's role as a musician in Saul's court (1Sm 16:14–23), as well as his many experiences as a shepherd, a soldier, and a king, make him a likely candidate for writing many of the psalms. Other psalms are attributed to the sons of Korah (Ps 42; 44–49; 84–85; 87–88), Asaph (Ps 50; 70–83), Solomon (Ps 72; 127), Heman the Ezrahite (Ps 88), Ethan the Ezrahite (Ps 89), and Moses (Ps 90).

MESSAGE AND PURPOSE

The unique themes, literary forms, and characteristics of each psalm contribute to a broader understanding of what it means to bring our whole selves to God. The responses of God's people in worship and prayer model how to relate to God in various life experiences. The book of Psalms also demonstrates God's sovereignty and goodness to His people in order to instill confidence in those who trust in Him. This record of how God's people responded to Him and to life in a broken world in worship and prayer demonstrates how seeking God in every circumstance restores our peace, joy, and hope

THE LENTEN SEASON AND THE PSALMS

Lent is a season of the Church calendar each year consisting of forty fasting days and six feasting Sundays that begin on Ash Wednesday and continue through Holy Saturday. During the season of Lent, we take intentional time to meditate on our deep need for a Savior as a way of preparing our hearts and minds for Easter.

For thousands of years, God's people have read and sung the psalms as a means of seeking, celebrating, lamenting, and resting in God's presence. The psalms remind us of who God is, show us who we are in light of Him, and connect us to God in the middle of a broken world. Whether it's our individual sin or the consequences of brokenness that are at work to push us away from God, the psalms give tangible language and images to realign our hearts to God's truth. And above all, they refocus our attention on the God who gave Himself so that we could draw near to Him both now and for eternity. This Lenten season, the book of Psalms will help us experience Lent from a place of worship—proclaiming who God is and letting gratitude for His sacrifice guide our contemplation.

IN THIS READING PLAN

Each day, we will read a few psalms and reflect on what stands out to us as we move through the Lenten season. Though each day's psalms will cover a variety of topics, a subtitle at the start of each day provides an overarching theme to have in mind as you read. A worksheet at the end of each day gives you space to ponder any questions, specific poetic imagery, or emotions that the day's reading might bring up for you. At the end of each week, we will connect with God through a guided prayer exercise with one of the psalms (we've provided an example prayer on page 46). The last four days of this reading plan turn to the final events of Holy Week—the Last Supper, the crucifixion, Jesus's burial, and the resurrection.

TIPS *for* READING PSALMS

READ EACH PSALM IN LIGHT OF ITS BROADER CONTEXT.

When reading Scripture, we want to be aware of both what was going on in the world of the author and how the passages are put together in the book. Read each psalm in its entirety, looking for clues that may connect it to other stories in the Old Testament. By understanding what the psalm meant to its original audience, we can uncover what it may mean for us today.

LOOK FOR METAPHORS, IMAGERY, AND OTHER PATTERNS IN EACH PSALM.

Many literary and poetic devices are used throughout the book of Psalms to communicate literal truth with abstract language, symbols, and stylistic choices. These devices help us comprehend supernatural, complex, or mysterious truths in relational terms. (See page 269 for definitions of common poetic devices.)

NOTICE HOW GOD IS DESCRIBED.

The book of Psalms informs what we know about God's power, character, and interactions with humanity. As you read, look for reminders of who God is and how we can respond to Him.

NOTICE HOW THE PSALMS REVEAL OUR NEED.

In the book of Psalms there is a repeated longing for redemption and restoration. The bleak language and imagery point toward the ultimate hope and fulfillment of these desires: Jesus Christ.

ALLOW YOURSELF TO BE SHAPED BY THE BOOK OF PSALMS.

The psalms have served as both prayers and songs of worship for the people of God for thousands of years. They invite us to abide with God on an emotional level within their weighty theological truths and moral expectations. Praying and singing the psalms allows us to develop new vocabulary in our conversations with God.

Salvation Belongs to the Lord

PSALMS 1–6

DAY 1 .... WEEK 1

Psalm 1

The Two Ways

1 How happy is the one who does not
walk in the advice of the wicked
or stand in the pathway with sinners
or sit in the company of mockers!
2 Instead, his delight is in the LORD's instruction,
and he meditates on it day and night.
3 He is like a tree planted beside flowing streams
that bears its fruit in its season,
and its leaf does not wither.
Whatever he does prospers.

4 The wicked are not like this;
instead, they are like chaff that the wind blows away.
5 Therefore the wicked will not stand up in the judgment,
nor sinners in the assembly of the righteous.

6 For the LORD watches over the way of the righteous,
but the way of the wicked leads to ruin.

Psalm 2

Coronation of the Son

1 Why do the nations rage
and the peoples plot in vain?
2 The kings of the earth take their stand,
and the rulers conspire together
against the LORD and his Anointed One:
3 "Let's tear off their chains
and throw their ropes off of us."

4 The one enthroned in heaven laughs;
the Lord ridicules them.
5 Then he speaks to them in his anger
and terrifies them in his wrath:
6 "I have installed my king
on Zion, my holy mountain."

7 I will declare the LORD's decree.
He said to me, "You are my Son;
today I have become your Father.
8 Ask of me,
and I will make the nations your inheritance
and the ends of the earth your possession.
9 You will break them with an iron scepter;
you will shatter them like pottery."

10 So now, kings, be wise;
receive instruction, you judges of the earth.
11 Serve the LORD with reverential awe
and rejoice with trembling.
12 Pay homage to the Son or he will be angry
and you will perish in your rebellion,
for his anger may ignite at any moment.
All who take refuge in him are happy.

Psalm 3

Confidence in Troubled Times

A PSALM OF DAVID WHEN HE FLED FROM HIS SON ABSALOM.

1 Lord, how my foes increase!
There are many who attack me.
2 Many say about me,
"There is no help for him in God." *Selah*

3 But you, Lord, are a shield around me,
my glory, and the one who lifts up my head.
4 I cry aloud to the Lord,
and he answers me from his holy mountain. *Selah*

5 I lie down and sleep;
I wake again because the Lord sustains me.
6 I will not be afraid of thousands of people
who have taken their stand against me on every side.

7 Rise up, Lord!
Save me, my God!
You strike all my enemies on the cheek;
you break the teeth of the wicked.
8 Salvation belongs to the Lord;
may your blessing be on your people. *Selah*

Psalm 4

A Night Prayer

FOR THE CHOIR DIRECTOR: WITH STRINGED INSTRUMENTS.
A PSALM OF DAVID.

1 Answer me when I call,
God, who vindicates me.
You freed me from affliction;
be gracious to me and hear my prayer.

2 How long, exalted ones, will my honor be insulted?
How long will you love what is worthless
and pursue a lie? *Selah*
3 Know that the Lord has set apart
the faithful for himself;
the Lord will hear when I call to him.
4 Be angry and do not sin;
reflect in your heart while on your bed and be silent. *Selah*

5 Offer sacrifices in righteousness
and trust in the LORD.

6 Many are asking, "Who can show us anything good?"
Let the light of your face shine on us, LORD.

7 You have put more joy in my heart
than they have when their grain and new wine abound.
8 I will both lie down and sleep in peace,
for you alone, LORD, make me live in safety.

Psalm 5

The Refuge of the Righteous

FOR THE CHOIR DIRECTOR: WITH THE FLUTES.
A PSALM OF DAVID.

1 Listen to my words, LORD;
consider my sighing.
2 Pay attention to the sound of my cry,
my King and my God,
for I pray to you.

3 In the morning, LORD, you hear my voice;
in the morning I plead my case to you and watch expectantly.

4 For you are not a God who delights in wickedness;
evil cannot dwell with you.
5 The boastful cannot stand in your sight;
you hate all evildoers.
6 You destroy those who tell lies;
the LORD abhors violent and treacherous people.

7 But I enter your house
by the abundance of your faithful love;
I bow down toward your holy temple
in reverential awe of you.
8 LORD, lead me in your righteousness
because of my adversaries;
make your way straight before me.

9 For there is nothing reliable in what they say;
destruction is within them;
their throat is an open grave;
they flatter with their tongues.
10 Punish them, God;
let them fall by their own schemes.
Drive them out because of their many crimes,
for they rebel against you.

11 But let all who take refuge in you rejoice;
let them shout for joy forever.
May you shelter them,
and may those who love your name boast about you.
12 For you, LORD, bless the righteous one;
you surround him with favor like a shield.

Psalm 6

A Prayer for Mercy

FOR THE CHOIR DIRECTOR: WITH STRINGED INSTRUMENTS,
ACCORDING TO *SHEMINITH*. A PSALM OF DAVID.

1 LORD, do not rebuke me in your anger;
do not discipline me in your wrath.
2 Be gracious to me, LORD, for I am weak;
heal me, LORD, for my bones are shaking;
3 my whole being is shaken with terror.
And you, LORD—how long?

4 Turn, LORD! Rescue me;
save me because of your faithful love.
5 For there is no remembrance of you in death;
who can thank you in Sheol?

6 I am weary from my groaning;
with my tears I dampen my bed
and drench my couch every night.
7 My eyes are swollen from grief;
they grow old because of all my enemies.

8 Depart from me, all evildoers,
for the LORD has heard the sound of my weeping.
9 The LORD has heard my plea for help;
the LORD accepts my prayer.
10 All my enemies will be ashamed and shake with terror;
they will turn back and suddenly be disgraced.

Daily Response

Date:

WHAT ATTRIBUTES *of* GOD STOOD OUT TO ME?

The psalms teach us about who God is and what He is like. List any aspects of God's character that stood out to you from these psalms.

HOW DO I CONNECT *with* THE HUMAN EXPERIENCES EXPRESSED *in* TODAY'S PSALMS?

The psalms were written by real people who encountered a diverse range of experiences and emotions. Use this space to reflect on places in the psalms that remind you of your own humanity.

Contextual markers

Take note of any places where each psalm indicates an author, occasion for its writing, or musical instructions.

Poetic devices or patterns

See the glossary on page 268 for a reminder of what each of these poetic elements is.

Words or phrases for further study

Some of the psalms may contain words or phrases you're unfamiliar with. List out any of those here, and before you look them up in other places, flip back to the glossary on page 268 to see if we've defined them for you!

HOW DO TODAY'S PSALMS GUIDE ME *in the* PRACTICES *of* LENT?

The book of Psalms gives us helpful language to move through Lent. As you reflect on who God is and the emotions these psalms evoke in you, how can you worship God through confession, lament, repentance, and/or praise today?

WHAT'S A VERSE *that* I WILL MEDITATE *on* TODAY?

DAY 2

Psalms 7–10

I WILL REJOICE *in*
YOUR SALVATION

Psalm 7

Prayer for Justice

A *SHIGGAION* OF DAVID, WHICH HE SANG TO THE LORD CONCERNING THE WORDS OF CUSH, A BENJAMINITE.

1 LORD my God, I seek refuge in you;
save me from all my pursuers and rescue me,
2 or they will tear me like a lion,
ripping me apart with no one to rescue me.

3 LORD my God, if I have done this,
if there is injustice on my hands,
4 if I have done harm to one at peace with me
or have plundered my adversary without cause,
5 may an enemy pursue and overtake me;
may he trample me to the ground
and leave my honor in the dust. *Selah*

6 Rise up, LORD, in your anger;
lift yourself up against the fury of my adversaries;
awake for me;
you have ordained a judgment.
7 Let the assembly of peoples gather around you;
take your seat on high over it.
8 The LORD judges the peoples;
vindicate me, LORD,
according to my righteousness and my integrity.

9 Let the evil of the wicked come to an end,
but establish the righteous.
The one who examines the thoughts and emotions
is a righteous God.
10 My shield is with God,
who saves the upright in heart.
11 God is a righteous judge
and a God who shows his wrath every day.

12 If anyone does not repent,
he will sharpen his sword;
he has strung his bow and made it ready.
13 He has prepared his deadly weapons;
he tips his arrows with fire.

14 See, the wicked one is pregnant with evil,
conceives trouble, and gives birth to deceit.
15 He dug a pit and hollowed it out
but fell into the hole he had made.
16 His trouble comes back on his own head;
his own violence comes down on top of his head.

17 I will thank the LORD for his righteousness;
I will sing about the name of the LORD Most High.

Psalm 8

God's Glory, Human Dignity

FOR THE CHOIR DIRECTOR: ON THE *GITTITH*.
A PSALM OF DAVID.

1 LORD, our Lord,
how magnificent is your name throughout the earth!
You have covered the heavens with your majesty.
2 From the mouths of infants and nursing babies,
you have established a stronghold
on account of your adversaries
in order to silence the enemy and the avenger.

3 When I observe your heavens,
the work of your fingers,
the moon and the stars,
which you set in place,
4 what is a human being that you remember him,
a son of man that you look after him?
5 You made him little less than God
and crowned him with glory and honor.
6 You made him ruler over the works of your hands;
you put everything under his feet:
7 all the sheep and oxen,
as well as the animals in the wild,
8 the birds of the sky,
and the fish of the sea
that pass through the currents of the seas.

9 LORD, our Lord,
how magnificent is your name throughout the earth!

Psalm 9

Celebration of God's Justice

FOR THE CHOIR DIRECTOR: ACCORDING TO *MUTH-LABBEN*.
A PSALM OF DAVID.

1 I will thank the LORD with all my heart;

I WILL DECLARE ALL YOUR
WONDROUS WORKS.

2 I will rejoice and boast about you;
I will sing about your name, Most High.

3 When my enemies retreat,
they stumble and perish before you.
4 For you have upheld my just cause;
you are seated on your throne as a righteous judge.
5 You have rebuked the nations:
You have destroyed the wicked;
you have erased their name forever and ever.
6 The enemy has come to eternal ruin;
you have uprooted the cities,
and the very memory of them has perished.

7 But the LORD sits enthroned forever;
he has established his throne for judgment.
8 And he judges the world with righteousness;
he executes judgment on the nations with fairness.
9 The LORD is a refuge for the persecuted,
a refuge in times of trouble.
10 Those who know your name trust in you
because you have not abandoned
those who seek you, LORD.

11 Sing to the LORD, who dwells in Zion;
proclaim his deeds among the nations.
12 For the one who seeks an accounting
for bloodshed remembers them;
he does not forget the cry of the oppressed.

13 Be gracious to me, LORD;
consider my affliction at the hands of those who hate me.

NOTES

Lift me up from the gates of death,
14 so that I may declare all your praises.
I will rejoice in your salvation
within the gates of Daughter Zion.

15 The nations have fallen into the pit they made;
their foot is caught in the net they have concealed.
16 The LORD has made himself known;
he has executed justice,
snaring the wicked
by the work of their hands. *Higgaion. Selah*

17 The wicked will return to Sheol—
all the nations that forget God.
18 For the needy will not always be forgotten;
the hope of the oppressed will not perish forever.

19 Rise up, LORD! Do not let mere humans prevail;
let the nations be judged in your presence.
20 Put terror in them, LORD;
let the nations know they are only humans. *Selah*

Psalm 10

Need for God's Justice

1 LORD, why do you stand so far away?
Why do you hide in times of trouble?
2 In arrogance the wicked relentlessly pursue their victims;
let them be caught in the schemes they have devised.

3 For the wicked one boasts about his own cravings;
the one who is greedy curses and despises the LORD.
4 In all his scheming,
the wicked person arrogantly thinks,
"There's no accountability,
since there's no God."
5 His ways are always secure;
your lofty judgments have no effect on him;
he scoffs at all his adversaries.
6 He says to himself, "I will never be moved—

from generation to generation I will be without calamity."
7 Cursing, deceit, and violence fill his mouth;
trouble and malice are under his tongue.
8 He waits in ambush near settlements;
he kills the innocent in secret places.
His eyes are on the lookout for the helpless;
9 he lurks in secret like a lion in a thicket.
He lurks in order to seize a victim;
he seizes a victim and drags him in his net.
10 So he is oppressed and beaten down;
helpless people fall because of the wicked one's strength.
11 He says to himself, "God has forgotten;
he hides his face and will never see."

12 Rise up, Lord God! Lift up your hand.
Do not forget the oppressed.
13 Why has the wicked person despised God?
He says to himself, "You will not demand an account."
14 But you yourself have seen trouble and grief,
observing it in order to take the matter into your hands.
The helpless one entrusts himself to you;
you are a helper of the fatherless.
15 Break the arm of the wicked, evil person,
until you look for his wickedness,
but it can't be found.

16 The Lord is King forever and ever;
the nations will perish from his land.
17 Lord, you have heard the desire of the humble;
you will strengthen their hearts.
You will listen carefully,
18 doing justice for the fatherless and the oppressed
so that mere humans from the earth may terrify them no more.

Daily Response

Date:

WHAT ATTRIBUTES *of* GOD STOOD OUT TO ME?

HOW DO I CONNECT *with* THE HUMAN EXPERIENCES EXPRESSED *in* TODAY'S PSALMS?

Contextual markers

Poetic devices or patterns

Words or phrases for further study

HOW DO TODAY'S PSALMS GUIDE ME *in the* PRACTICES *of* LENT?

WHAT'S A VERSE *that* I WILL MEDITATE *on* TODAY?

PSALMS 11–16

I HAVE TRUSTED *in* YOUR FAITHFUL LOVE

But I have trusted in your faithful love; my heart will rejoice in your deliverance.

Psalm 13:5

Psalm 11

Refuge in the Lord

FOR THE CHOIR DIRECTOR. OF DAVID.

1 I have taken refuge in the LORD.
How can you say to me,
"Escape to the mountains like a bird!
2 For look, the wicked string bows;
they put their arrows on bowstrings
to shoot from the shadows at the upright in heart.
3 When the foundations are destroyed,
what can the righteous do?"

4 The LORD is in his holy temple;
the LORD—his throne is in heaven.
His eyes watch;
his gaze examines everyone.
5 The LORD examines the righteous,
but he hates the wicked
and those who love violence.
6 Let him rain burning coals and sulfur on the wicked;
let a scorching wind be the portion in their cup.
7 For the LORD is righteous; he loves righteous deeds.
The upright will see his face.

Psalm 12

Oppression by the Wicked

FOR THE CHOIR DIRECTOR: ACCORDING TO *SHEMINITH*.
A PSALM OF DAVID.

1 Help, LORD, for no faithful one remains;
the loyal have disappeared from the human race.
2 They lie to one another;
they speak with flattering lips and deceptive hearts.
3 May the LORD cut off all flattering lips
and the tongue that speaks boastfully.
4 They say, "Through our tongues we have power;
our lips are our own—who can be our master?"

5 "Because of the devastation of the needy
and the groaning of the poor,
I will now rise up," says the LORD.
"I will provide safety for the one who longs for it."

6 The words of the LORD are pure words,
like silver refined in an earthen furnace,
purified seven times.

7 You, LORD, will guard us;
you will protect us from this generation forever.
8 The wicked prowl all around,
and what is worthless is exalted by the human race.

Psalm 13

A Plea for Deliverance

FOR THE CHOIR DIRECTOR. A PSALM OF DAVID.

1 How long, LORD? Will you forget me forever?
How long will you hide your face from me?
2 How long will I store up anxious concerns within me,
agony in my mind every day?
How long will my enemy dominate me?

3 Consider me and answer, LORD my God.
Restore brightness to my eyes;
otherwise, I will sleep in death.
4 My enemy will say, "I have triumphed over him,"
and my foes will rejoice because I am shaken.

5 But I have trusted in your faithful love;
my heart will rejoice in your deliverance.
6 I will sing to the LORD
because he has treated me generously.

Psalm 14

A Portrait of Sinners

FOR THE CHOIR DIRECTOR. OF DAVID.

1 The fool says in his heart, "There's no God."
They are corrupt; they do vile deeds.
There is no one who does good.
2 The LORD looks down from heaven on the human race
to see if there is one who is wise,

one who seeks God.
[3] All have turned away;
all alike have become corrupt.
There is no one who does good,
not even one.

[4] Will evildoers never understand?
They consume my people as they consume bread;
they do not call on the LORD.

[5] Then they will be filled with dread,
for God is with those who are righteous.
[6] You sinners frustrate the plans of the oppressed,
but the LORD is his refuge.

[7] Oh, that Israel's deliverance would come from Zion!
When the LORD restores the fortunes of his people,
let Jacob rejoice, let Israel be glad.

Psalm 15

A Description of the Godly

A PSALM OF DAVID.

[1] LORD, who can dwell in your tent?
Who can live on your holy mountain?

[2] The one who lives blamelessly, practices righteousness,
and acknowledges the truth in his heart—
[3] who does not slander with his tongue,
who does not harm his friend
or discredit his neighbor,
[4] who despises the one rejected by the LORD
but honors those who fear the LORD,
who keeps his word whatever the cost,
[5] who does not lend his silver at interest
or take a bribe against the innocent—
the one who does these things will never be shaken.

Psalm 16

Confidence in the Lord

A *MIKTAM* OF DAVID.

[1] Protect me, God, for I take refuge in you.
[2] I said to the LORD, "You are my Lord;
I have nothing good besides you."
[3] As for the holy people who are in the land,
they are the noble ones.
All my delight is in them.
[4] The sorrows of those who take another god
for themselves will multiply;
I will not pour out their drink offerings of blood,
and I will not speak their names with my lips.

[5] LORD, you are my portion
and my cup of blessing;
you hold my future.
[6] The boundary lines have fallen for me
in pleasant places;
indeed, I have a beautiful inheritance.

[7] I will bless the LORD who counsels me—
even at night when my thoughts trouble me.
[8] I always let the LORD guide me.
Because he is at my right hand,
I will not be shaken.

[9] THEREFORE MY HEART IS GLAD
AND MY WHOLE BEING REJOICES;
MY BODY ALSO RESTS SECURELY.

[10] For you will not abandon me to Sheol;
you will not allow your faithful one to see decay.
[11] You reveal the path of life to me;
in your presence is abundant joy;
at your right hand are eternal pleasures.

Daily Response

Date:

WHAT ATTRIBUTES *of* GOD STOOD OUT TO ME?

HOW DO I CONNECT *with* THE HUMAN EXPERIENCES EXPRESSED *in* TODAY'S PSALMS?

Contextual markers

Poetic devices or patterns

Words or phrases for further study

HOW DO TODAY'S PSALMS GUIDE ME *in the* PRACTICES *of* LENT?

WHAT'S A VERSE *that* I WILL MEDITATE *on* TODAY?

SAVIOR OF ALL WHO SEEK REFUGE

Psalms 17–18

DISPLAY *the* WONDERS *of* YOUR FAITHFUL LOVE, SAVIOR *of* ALL WHO SEEK REFUGE *from* THOSE WHO REBEL AGAINST YOUR RIGHT HAND.

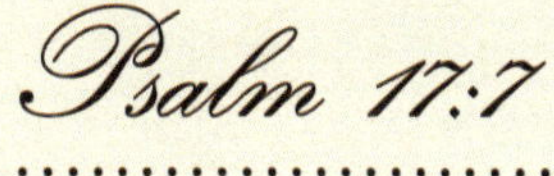

DAY 4

WEEK 1

Psalm 17

A Prayer for Protection

A PRAYER OF DAVID.

1 LORD, hear a just cause;
pay attention to my cry;
listen to my prayer—
from lips free of deceit.
2 Let my vindication come from you,
for you see what is right.
3 You have tested my heart;
you have examined me at night.
You have tried me and found nothing evil;
I have determined that my mouth will not sin.
4 Concerning what people do:
by the words from your lips
I have avoided the ways of the violent.
5 My steps are on your paths;
my feet have not slipped.

6 I call on you, God,
because you will answer me;
listen closely to me; hear what I say.
7 Display the wonders of your faithful love,
Savior of all who seek refuge
from those who rebel against your right hand.
8 Protect me as the pupil of your eye;
hide me in the shadow of your wings
9 from the wicked who treat me violently,
my deadly enemies who surround me.

10 They are uncaring;
their mouths speak arrogantly.
11 They advance against me; now they surround me.
They are determined
to throw me to the ground.
12 They are like a lion eager to tear,
like a young lion lurking in ambush.

13 Rise up, LORD!
Confront him; bring him down.
With your sword, save me from the wicked.
14 With your hand, LORD, save me from men,
from men of the world
whose portion is in this life:
You fill their bellies with what you have in store;
their sons are satisfied,
and they leave their surplus to their children.

15 But I will see your face in righteousness;
when I awake, I will be satisfied with your presence.

Psalm 18

Praise for Deliverance

FOR THE CHOIR DIRECTOR. OF THE SERVANT OF THE LORD, DAVID, WHO SPOKE THE WORDS OF THIS SONG TO THE LORD ON THE DAY THE LORD RESCUED HIM FROM THE GRASP OF ALL HIS ENEMIES AND FROM THE POWER OF SAUL. HE SAID:

1 I love you, LORD, my strength.
2 The LORD is my rock,
my fortress, and my deliverer,
my God, my rock where I seek refuge,
my shield and the horn of my salvation,
my stronghold.
3 I called to the LORD, who is worthy of praise,
and I was saved from my enemies.

4 The ropes of death were wrapped around me;
the torrents of destruction terrified me.
5 The ropes of Sheol entangled me;
the snares of death confronted me.
6 I called to the LORD in my distress,
and I cried to my God for help.
From his temple he heard my voice,
and my cry to him reached his ears.

7 Then the earth shook and quaked;
the foundations of the mountains trembled;
they shook because he burned with anger.
8 Smoke rose from his nostrils,
and consuming fire came from his mouth;
coals were set ablaze by it.
9 He bent the heavens and came down,
total darkness beneath his feet.
10 He rode on a cherub and flew,
soaring on the wings of the wind.

11 He made darkness his hiding place,
dark storm clouds his canopy around him.
12 From the radiance of his presence,
his clouds swept onward with hail and blazing coals.
13 The LORD thundered from heaven;
the Most High made his voice heard.
14 He shot his arrows and scattered them;
he hurled lightning bolts and routed them.
15 The depths of the sea became visible,
the foundations of the world were exposed,
at your rebuke, LORD,
at the blast of the breath of your nostrils.

16 He reached down from on high
and took hold of me;
he pulled me out of deep water.
17 He rescued me from my powerful enemy
and from those who hated me,
for they were too strong for me.
18 They confronted me in the day of my calamity,
but the LORD was my support.
19 He brought me out to a spacious place;
he rescued me because he delighted in me.

20 The LORD rewarded me
according to my righteousness;
he repaid me
according to the cleanness of my hands.
21 For I have kept the ways of the LORD
and have not turned from my God to wickedness.
22 Indeed, I let all his ordinances guide me
and have not disregarded his statutes.
23 I was blameless toward him
and kept myself from my iniquity.
24 So the LORD repaid me
according to my righteousness,
according to the cleanness of my hands in his sight.

25 With the faithful
you prove yourself faithful,
with the blameless
you prove yourself blameless,
26 with the pure
you prove yourself pure,

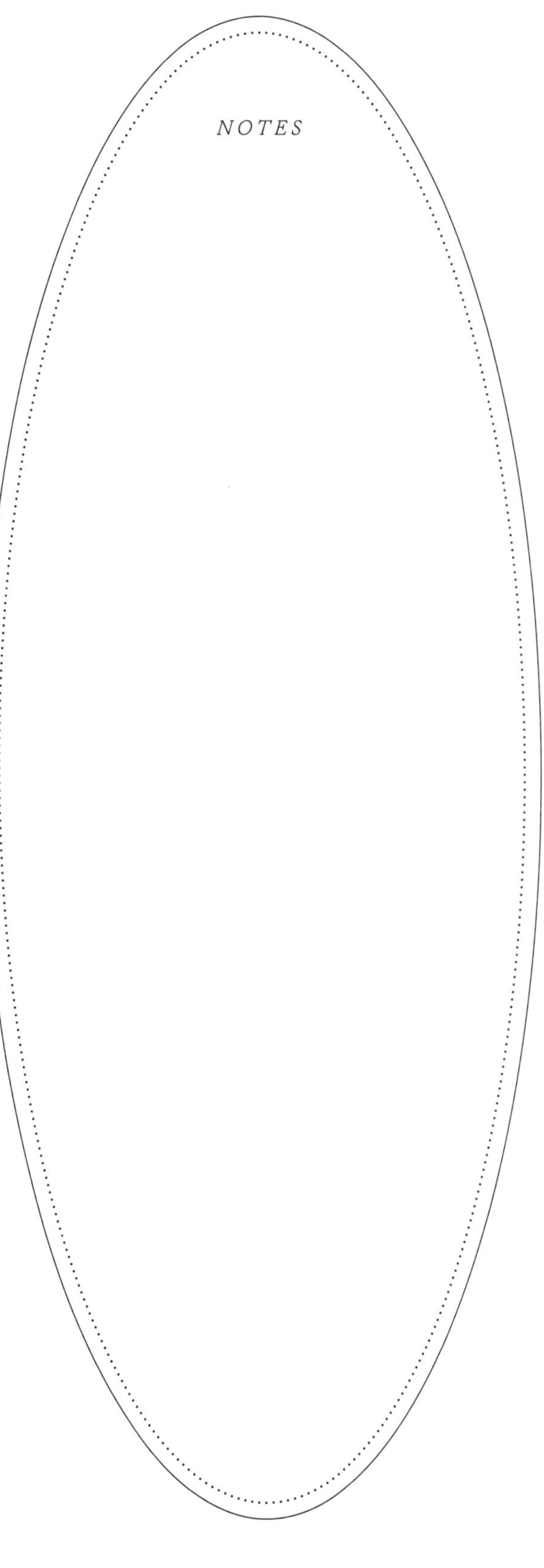

but with the crooked
you prove yourself shrewd.
27 For you rescue an oppressed people,
but you humble those with haughty eyes.
28 LORD, you light my lamp;
my God illuminates my darkness.
29 With you I can attack a barricade,
and with my God I can leap over a wall.

30 God—his way is perfect;
the word of the LORD is pure.
He is a shield to all who take refuge in him.
31 For who is God besides the LORD?
And who is a rock? Only our God.
32 God—he clothes me with strength
and makes my way perfect.
33 He makes my feet like the feet of a deer
and sets me securely on the heights.
34 He trains my hands for war;
my arms can bend a bow of bronze.
35 You have given me the shield of your salvation;
your right hand upholds me,
and your humility exalts me.
36 You make a spacious place beneath me for my steps,
and my ankles do not give way.

37 I pursue my enemies and overtake them;
I do not turn back until they are wiped out.
38 I crush them, and they cannot get up;
they fall beneath my feet.
39 You have clothed me with strength for battle;
you subdue my adversaries beneath me.
40 You have made my enemies retreat before me;
I annihilate those who hate me.
41 They cry for help, but there is no one to save them—
they cry to the LORD, but he does not answer them.
42 I pulverize them like dust before the wind;
I trample them like mud in the streets.

43 You have freed me from the feuds among the people;
you have appointed me the head of nations;
a people I had not known serve me.
44 Foreigners submit to me cringing;
as soon as they hear they obey me.
45 Foreigners lose heart
and come trembling from their fortifications.

46 THE LORD LIVES—BLESSED
BE MY ROCK!
THE GOD OF MY SALVATION
IS EXALTED.

47 God—he grants me vengeance
and subdues peoples under me.
48 He frees me from my enemies.
You exalt me above my adversaries;
you rescue me from violent men.
49 Therefore I will give thanks to you among the
nations, LORD;
I will sing praises about your name.
50 He gives great victories to his king;
he shows loyalty to his anointed,
to David and his descendants forever.

Daily Response

Date:

WHAT ATTRIBUTES *of* GOD STOOD OUT TO ME?

HOW DO I CONNECT *with* THE HUMAN EXPERIENCES EXPRESSED *in* TODAY'S PSALMS?

Contextual markers

Poetic devices or patterns

Words or phrases for further study

HOW DO TODAY'S PSALMS GUIDE ME *in the* PRACTICES *of* LENT?

WHAT'S A VERSE *that* I WILL MEDITATE *on* TODAY?

PSALMS 19–22

DAY
5

WEEK
1

LORD, DON'T BE FAR

Psalms 19

The Witness of Creation and Scripture
FOR THE CHOIR DIRECTOR. A PSALM OF DAVID.

1 The heavens declare the glory of God,
and the expanse proclaims the work of his hands.
2 Day after day they pour out speech;
night after night they communicate knowledge.
3 There is no speech; there are no words;
their voice is not heard.
4 Their message has gone out to the whole earth,
and their words to the ends of the world.
In the heavens he has pitched a tent for the sun.
5 It is like a bridegroom coming from his home;
it rejoices like an athlete running a course.
6 It rises from one end of the heavens
and circles to their other end;
nothing is hidden from its heat.

7 The instruction of the LORD is perfect,
renewing one's life;
the testimony of the LORD is trustworthy,
making the inexperienced wise.
8 The precepts of the LORD are right,
making the heart glad;
the command of the LORD is radiant,
making the eyes light up.
9 The fear of the LORD is pure,
enduring forever;
the ordinances of the LORD are reliable
and altogether righteous.
10 They are more desirable than gold—
than an abundance of pure gold;
and sweeter than honey
dripping from a honeycomb.
11 In addition, your servant is warned by them,
and in keeping them there is an abundant reward.

12 Who perceives his unintentional sins?
Cleanse me from my hidden faults.
13 Moreover, keep your servant from willful sins;
do not let them rule me.
Then I will be blameless
and cleansed from blatant rebellion.
14 May the words of my mouth
and the meditation of my heart
be acceptable to you,
LORD, my rock and my Redeemer.

Psalm 20

Deliverance in Battle
FOR THE CHOIR DIRECTOR. A PSALM OF DAVID.

1 May the LORD answer you in a day of trouble;
may the name of Jacob's God protect you.
2 May he send you help from the sanctuary
and sustain you from Zion.
3 May he remember all your offerings
and accept your burnt offering. *Selah*

4 May he give you what your heart desires
and fulfill your whole purpose.

5 Let us shout for joy at your victory
and lift the banner in the name of our God.
May the LORD fulfill all your requests.

6 Now I know that the LORD gives victory to his anointed;
he will answer him from his holy heaven
with mighty victories from his right hand.
7 Some take pride in chariots, and others in horses,
but we take pride in the name of the LORD our God.
8 They collapse and fall,
but we rise and stand firm.
9 LORD, give victory to the king!
May he answer us on the day that we call.

Psalm 21

The King's Victory

FOR THE CHOIR DIRECTOR. A PSALM OF DAVID.

1 LORD, the king finds joy in your strength.
How greatly he rejoices in your victory!
2 You have given him his heart's desire
and have not denied the request of his lips. *Selah*
3 For you meet him with rich blessings;
you place a crown of pure gold on his head.
4 He asked you for life, and you gave it to him—
length of days forever and ever.
5 His glory is great through your victory;
you confer majesty and splendor on him.
6 You give him blessings forever;
you cheer him with joy in your presence.
7 For the king relies on the LORD;
through the faithful love of the Most High
he is not shaken.

8 Your hand will capture all your enemies;
your right hand will seize those who hate you.
9 You will make them burn
like a fiery furnace when you appear;
the LORD will engulf them in his wrath,
and fire will devour them.
10 You will wipe their progeny from the earth
and their offspring from the human race.
11 Though they intend to harm you
and devise a wicked plan, they will not prevail.

NOTES

12 Instead, you will put them to flight
when you ready your bowstrings to shoot at them.

13 BE EXALTED, LORD, IN YOUR STRENGTH;
WE WILL SING AND PRAISE YOUR MIGHT.

Psalm 22

From Suffering to Praise

FOR THE CHOIR DIRECTOR: ACCORDING TO "THE DEER OF THE DAWN."
A PSALM OF DAVID.

1 My God, my God, why have you abandoned me?
Why are you so far from my deliverance
and from my words of groaning?
2 My God, I cry by day, but you do not answer,
by night, yet I have no rest.
3 But you are holy,
enthroned on the praises of Israel.
4 Our ancestors trusted in you;
they trusted, and you rescued them.
5 They cried to you and were set free;
they trusted in you and were not disgraced.

6 But I am a worm and not a man,
scorned by mankind and despised by people.
7 Everyone who sees me mocks me;
they sneer and shake their heads:
8 "He relies on the Lord;
let him save him;
let the Lord rescue him,
since he takes pleasure in him."

9 It was you who brought me out of the womb,
making me secure at my mother's breast.
10 I was given over to you at birth;
you have been my God from my mother's womb.

11 Don't be far from me, because distress is near
and there's no one to help.

12 Many bulls surround me;
strong ones of Bashan encircle me.
13 They open their mouths against me—

lions, mauling and roaring.
14 I am poured out like water,
and all my bones are disjointed;
my heart is like wax,
melting within me.
15 My strength is dried up like baked clay;
my tongue sticks to the roof of my mouth.
You put me into the dust of death.
16 For dogs have surrounded me;
a gang of evildoers has closed in on me;
they pierced my hands and my feet.
17 I can count all my bones;
people look and stare at me.
18 They divided my garments among themselves,
and they cast lots for my clothing.

19 But you, LORD, don't be far away.
My strength, come quickly to help me.
20 Rescue my life from the sword,
my only life from the power of these dogs.
21 Save me from the lion's mouth,
from the horns of wild oxen.
You answered me!
22 I will proclaim your name to my brothers and sisters;
I will praise you in the assembly.
23 You who fear the LORD, praise him!
All you descendants of Jacob, honor him!
All you descendants of Israel, revere him!
24 For he has not despised or abhorred
the torment of the oppressed.
He did not hide his face from him
but listened when he cried to him for help.

25 I will give praise in the great assembly
because of you;
I will fulfill my vows
before those who fear you.
26 The humble will eat and be satisfied;
those who seek the LORD will praise him.
May your hearts live forever!

27 All the ends of the earth will remember
and turn to the LORD.
All the families of the nations
will bow down before you,
28 for kingship belongs to the LORD;
he rules the nations.
29 All who prosper on earth will eat and bow down;
all those who go down to the dust
will kneel before him—
even the one who cannot preserve his life.
30 Their descendants will serve him;
the next generation will be told about the Lord.
31 They will come and declare his righteousness;
to a people yet to be born
they will declare what he has done.

Daily Response

Date:

WHAT ATTRIBUTES *of* GOD STOOD OUT TO ME?

HOW DO I CONNECT *with* THE HUMAN EXPERIENCES EXPRESSED *in* TODAY'S PSALMS?

Contextual markers

Poetic devices or patterns

Words or phrases for further study

HOW DO TODAY'S PSALMS GUIDE ME *in the* PRACTICES *of* LENT?

WHAT'S A VERSE *that* I WILL MEDITATE *on* TODAY?

Example *Response*

Practicing the art of prayer is one of the great rewards of following Jesus over the course of a lifetime. The psalms themselves can be one of our greatest assets in guiding our discipline of prayer. At the end of each week, you'll find space to respond in prayer with a psalm from that week's readings. As you read the psalm, allow the words of Scripture to guide your prayer, talking to the Lord about whatever the psalm brings to mind. Here you'll find an example prayer for this exercise. And then on the following page you'll have space to write your own prayer.

Psalm 8

God's Glory, Human Dignity

FOR THE CHOIR DIRECTOR: ON THE *GITTITH*.
A PSALM OF DAVID.

Today I am especially thankful that you are God and I am not. I need help living that out today as I stumble in my ongoing need for control over my life.

1 LORD, our Lord,
how magnificent is your name throughout the earth!
You have covered the heavens with your majesty.

Thank you Lord for the work you're doing through my church's missionaries. Your name really is seen as magnificent throughout the earth.

2 From the mouths of infants and nursing babies,
you have established a stronghold
on account of your adversaries
in order to silence the enemy and the avenger.

3 When I observe your heavens,
the work of your fingers,
the moon and the stars,
which you set in place,

I so often forget that you are the one holding it all together, from everything I can touch to the things that I can only see like the moon and stars.

4 what is a human being that you remember him,
a son of man that you look after him?

You've continued to remind me how you remember me. I haven't always felt that way. For my friends that are doubting this truth today, fill them with the same assurance you have given me.

5 You made him little less than God
and crowned him with glory and honor.

As I work today, help me to be reminded of my unique role. I may not be tending animals today, but I know I'm living this command as I step into my office and work with excellence. I'm thankful to reflect your image in that way.

6 You made him ruler over the works of your hands;
you put everything under his feet:

I also can't help but to think of Jesus as I read this psalm. Jesus, you are Lord over all – from your followers to your enemies.

7 all the sheep and oxen,
as well as the animals in the wild,

8 the birds of the sky,
and the fish of the sea
that pass through the currents of the seas.

Lord, nothing is out of your reach. And even still, you've entrusted us with caring for this earth.

9 LORD, our Lord,
how magnificent is your name
throughout the earth!

My life can echo these words today. Your name is magnificent to me, in my life. Thank you for giving me the faith to believe that. Help my family to see evidence of that in me throughout our day.

Week One *Response*

Use Psalm 8 to respond in prayer, allowing the words of Scripture to guide your prayer. Talk to the Lord about whatever the psalm brings to mind. Refer back to the example on page 46 if you need to.

Psalm 8

God's Glory, Human Dignity

FOR THE CHOIR DIRECTOR: ON THE *GITTITH.*
A PSALM OF DAVID.

1 LORD, our Lord,
how magnificent is your name throughout the earth!
You have covered the heavens with your majesty.

2 From the mouths of infants and nursing babies,
you have established a stronghold
on account of your adversaries
in order to silence the enemy and the avenger.

3 When I observe your heavens,
the work of your fingers,
the moon and the stars,
which you set in place,

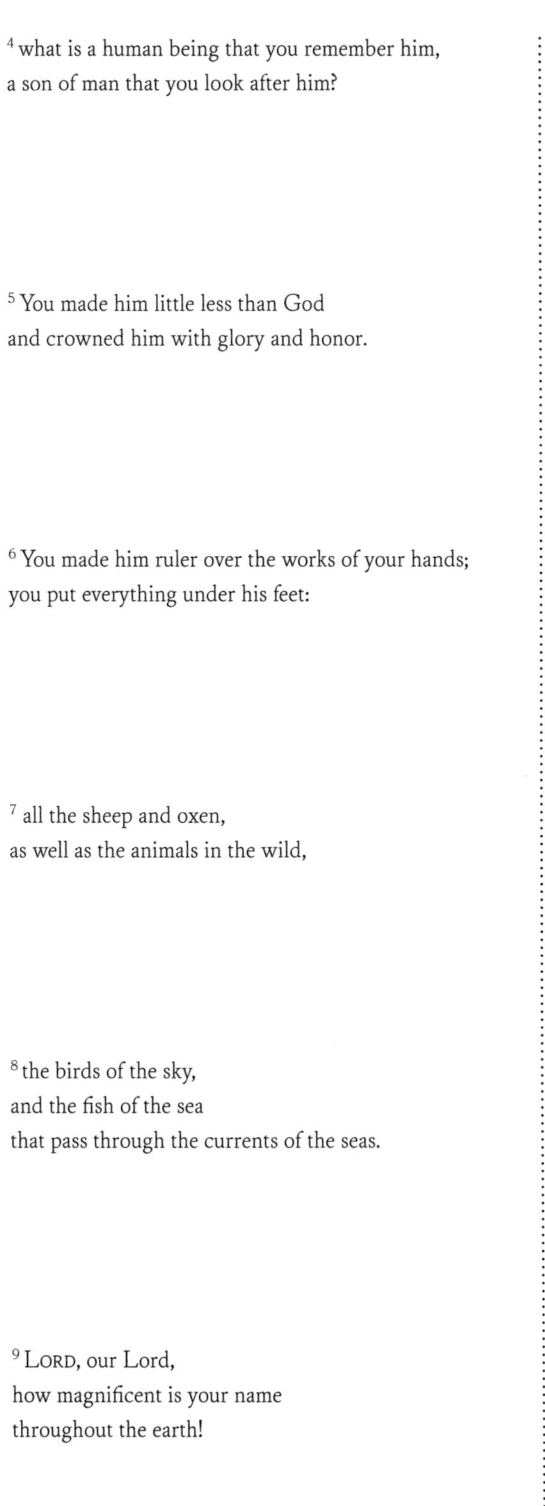

4 what is a human being that you remember him,
a son of man that you look after him?

5 You made him little less than God
and crowned him with glory and honor.

6 You made him ruler over the works of your hands;
you put everything under his feet:

7 all the sheep and oxen,
as well as the animals in the wild,

8 the birds of the sky,
and the fish of the sea
that pass through the currents of the seas.

9 LORD, our Lord,
how magnificent is your name
throughout the earth!

GRACE *Day*

TAKE EACH SATURDAY *to* CATCH UP ON YOUR READING, PRAY, *and* REST *in the* PRESENCE *of the* LORD *with* PASSAGES *from* SCRIPTURE THAT WE TRADITIONALLY READ DURING *the* LENTEN SEASON.

Even now—
this is the LORD's declaration—
turn to me with all your heart,
with fasting, weeping, and mourning.
Tear your hearts,
not just your clothes,
and return to the LORD your God.
For he is gracious and compassionate,
slow to anger, abounding in faithful love,
and he relents from sending disaster.

JOEL 2:12–13

DAY 7 - WEEK 1

WEEKLY TRUTH

SCRIPTURE IS GOD BREATHED *and* TRUE.
WHEN WE MEMORIZE IT, WE CARRY HIS WORD
with US WHEREVER WE GO.

Hallel psalms, coming from the Hebrew word meaning "to praise," are individual psalms or groups of psalms traditionally used during celebratory seasons of the Jewish calendar. While there are many Hallel psalms, Psalms 113–118 are known specifically as the "Egyptian Hallel" (a reference to Ps 114:1) and were recited, sung, or prayed in Jewish homes to commemorate the Passover.

Each Sunday during this plan, we will read a different Hallel psalm and memorize one of its verses.

This week, memorize Psalm 113:3 as you meditate on the psalm as a whole.

Psalm 113

Praise to the Merciful God

1 Hallelujah!
Give praise, servants of the LORD;
praise the name of the LORD.
2 Let the name of the LORD be blessed
both now and forever.
3 From the rising of the sun to its setting,
let the name of the LORD be praised.

4 The LORD is exalted above all the nations,
his glory above the heavens.
5 Who is like the LORD our God—
the one enthroned on high,
6 who stoops down to look
on the heavens and the earth?
7 He raises the poor from the dust
and lifts the needy from the trash heap
8 in order to seat them with nobles—
with the nobles of his people.
9 He gives the childless woman a household,
making her the joyful mother of children.
Hallelujah!

SEE TIPS FOR MEMORIZING SCRIPTURE ON PAGE 272.

PSALMS 23–29

MY LIGHT *and* MY SALVATION

The LORD is my light and my salvation—whom should I fear? The LORD is the stronghold of my life—whom should I dread?

Psalm 27:1

Psalm 23

The Good Shepherd

A PSALM OF DAVID.

1 The LORD is my shepherd;
I have what I need.
2 He lets me lie down in green pastures;
he leads me beside quiet waters.
3 He renews my life;
he leads me along the right paths
for his name's sake.
4 Even when I go through the darkest valley,
I fear no danger,
for you are with me;
your rod and your staff—they comfort me.

5 You prepare a table before me
in the presence of my enemies;
you anoint my head with oil;
my cup overflows.
6 Only goodness and faithful love will pursue me
all the days of my life,
and I will dwell in the house of the LORD
as long as I live.

Psalm 24

The King of Glory

A PSALM OF DAVID.

1 The earth and everything in it,
the world and its inhabitants,
belong to the LORD;
2 for he laid its foundation on the seas
and established it on the rivers.

3 Who may ascend the mountain of the LORD?
Who may stand in his holy place?
4 The one who has clean hands and a pure heart,
who has not appealed to what is false,
and who has not sworn deceitfully.
5 He will receive blessing from the LORD,
and righteousness from the God of his salvation.
6 Such is the generation of those who inquire of him,
who seek the face of the God of Jacob. *Selah*

7 Lift up your heads, you gates!
Rise up, ancient doors!
Then the King of glory will come in.
8 Who is this King of glory?
The LORD, strong and mighty,
the LORD, mighty in battle.
9 Lift up your heads, you gates!
Rise up, ancient doors!
Then the King of glory will come in.
10 Who is he, this King of glory?
The LORD of Armies,
he is the King of glory. *Selah*

Psalm 25

Dependence on the Lord

OF DAVID.

1 LORD, I appeal to you.
2 My God, I trust in you.
Do not let me be disgraced;
do not let my enemies gloat over me.
3 No one who waits for you
will be disgraced;
those who act treacherously without cause
will be disgraced.

4 Make your ways known to me, LORD;
teach me your paths.
5 Guide me in your truth and teach me,
for you are the God of my salvation;
I wait for you all day long.
6 Remember, LORD, your compassion
and your faithful love,
for they have existed from antiquity.
7 Do not remember the sins of my youth

or my acts of rebellion;
in keeping with your faithful love, remember me
because of your goodness, LORD.

8 The LORD is good and upright;
therefore he shows sinners the way.
9 He leads the humble in what is right
and teaches them his way.
10 All the LORD's ways show faithful love and truth
to those who keep his covenant and decrees.
11 LORD, for the sake of your name,
forgive my iniquity, for it is immense.

12 Who is this person who fears the LORD?
He will show him the way he should choose.
13 He will live a good life,
and his descendants will inherit the land.
14 The secret counsel of the LORD
is for those who fear him,
and he reveals his covenant to them.
15 My eyes are always on the LORD,
for he will pull my feet out of the net.

16 Turn to me and be gracious to me,
for I am alone and afflicted.
17 The distresses of my heart increase;
bring me out of my sufferings.
18 Consider my affliction and trouble,
and forgive all my sins.
19 Consider my enemies; they are numerous,
and they hate me violently.
20 Guard me and rescue me;
do not let me be disgraced,
for I take refuge in you.
21 May integrity and what is right
watch over me,
for I wait for you.

22 God, redeem Israel, from all its distresses.

Psalm 26

Prayer for Vindication

OF DAVID.

1 Vindicate me, LORD,
because I have lived with integrity
and have trusted in the LORD without wavering.
2 Test me, LORD, and try me;
examine my heart and mind.
3 For your faithful love guides me,
and I live by your truth.

4 I do not sit with the worthless
or associate with hypocrites.
5 I hate a crowd of evildoers,
and I do not sit with the wicked.
6 I wash my hands in innocence
and go around your altar, LORD,
7 raising my voice in thanksgiving
and telling about your wondrous works.

8 LORD, I love the house where you dwell,
the place where your glory resides.
9 Do not destroy me along with sinners,
or my life along with men of bloodshed
10 in whose hands are evil schemes
and whose right hands are filled with bribes.

11 But I live with integrity;
redeem me and be gracious to me.
12 My foot stands on level ground;
I will bless the LORD in the assemblies.

Psalm 27

My Stronghold

OF DAVID.

1 The LORD is my light and my salvation—
whom should I fear?
The LORD is the stronghold of my life—

whom should I dread?
2 When evildoers came against me to devour my flesh,
my foes and my enemies stumbled and fell.
3 Though an army deploys against me,
my heart will not be afraid;
though a war breaks out against me,
I will still be confident.

4 I have asked one thing from the LORD;
it is what I desire:
to dwell in the house of the LORD
all the days of my life,
gazing on the beauty of the LORD
and seeking him in his temple.
5 For he will conceal me in his shelter
in the day of adversity;
he will hide me under the cover of his tent;
he will set me high on a rock.
6 Then my head will be high
above my enemies around me;
I will offer sacrifices in his tent with shouts of joy.
I will sing and make music to the LORD.

7 LORD, hear my voice when I call;
be gracious to me and answer me.
8 My heart says this about you:
"Seek his face."
LORD, I will seek your face.
9 Do not hide your face from me;
do not turn your servant away in anger.
You have been my helper;
do not leave me or abandon me,
God of my salvation.
10 Even if my father and mother abandon me,
the LORD cares for me.

11 Because of my adversaries,
show me your way, LORD,
and lead me on a level path.

NOTES

12 Do not give me over to the will of my foes,
for false witnesses rise up against me,
breathing violence.

13 I am certain that I will see the LORD's goodness
in the land of the living.
14 Wait for the LORD;
be strong, and let your heart be courageous.
Wait for the LORD.

Psalm 28

My Strength

OF DAVID.

1 LORD, I call to you;
my rock, do not be deaf to me.
If you remain silent to me,
I will be like those going down to the Pit.
2 Listen to the sound of my pleading
when I cry to you for help,
when I lift up my hands
toward your holy sanctuary.

3 Do not drag me away with the wicked,
with the evildoers,
who speak in friendly ways with their neighbors
while malice is in their hearts.
4 Repay them according to what they have done—
according to the evil of their deeds.
Repay them according to the work of their hands;
give them back what they deserve.
5 Because they do not consider
what the LORD has done
or the work of his hands,
he will tear them down and not rebuild them.

6 Blessed be the LORD,
for he has heard the sound of my pleading.
7 The LORD is my strength and my shield;
my heart trusts in him, and I am helped.
Therefore my heart celebrates,
and I give thanks to him with my song.

8 The LORD is the strength of his people;
he is a stronghold of salvation for his anointed.
9 Save your people, bless your possession,
shepherd them, and carry them forever.

Psalm 29

The Voice of the Lord

A PSALM OF DAVID.

1 Ascribe to the LORD, you heavenly beings,
ascribe to the LORD glory and strength.
2 Ascribe to the LORD the glory due his name;
worship the LORD
in the splendor of his holiness.

3 The voice of the LORD is above the waters.
The God of glory thunders—
the LORD, above the vast water,
4 the voice of the LORD in power,
the voice of the LORD in splendor.
5 The voice of the LORD breaks the cedars;
the LORD shatters the cedars of Lebanon.
6 He makes Lebanon skip like a calf,
and Sirion, like a young wild ox.
7 The voice of the LORD flashes flames of fire.
8 The voice of the LORD shakes the wilderness;
the LORD shakes the wilderness of Kadesh.
9 The voice of the LORD makes the deer give birth
and strips the woodlands bare.
In his temple all cry, "Glory!"

10 The LORD sits enthroned over the flood;
the LORD sits enthroned, King forever.
11 The LORD gives his people strength;
the LORD blesses his people with peace.

Daily Response

Date:

WHAT ATTRIBUTES *of* GOD STOOD OUT TO ME?

HOW DO I CONNECT *with* THE HUMAN EXPERIENCES EXPRESSED *in* TODAY'S PSALMS?

Contextual markers

Poetic devices or patterns

Words or phrases for further study

HOW DO TODAY'S PSALMS GUIDE ME *in the* PRACTICES *of* LENT?

WHAT'S A VERSE *that* I WILL MEDITATE *on* TODAY?

FLORAL CLAY MOLDS

Supplies

- Wax paper
- 15 lbs white, air-dry clay
- Clay wire cutter
- Rolling pin
- Square or spring-form cake pan, picture frame, etc. (to function as base for mold)
- Fresh flowers and greenery
- Brayer
- 8 lbs Plaster of Paris white plaster
- Bucket
- Gloves

To Create Mold

(These instructions use a square cake pan to create the mold, but you can adapt them to fit whatever mold you decide to use!)

Tape down wax paper to protect work surface.

Slice off portion of clay using wire cutter.

Roll out clay until it is larger than cake pan and between ¼-inch and ½-inch thick. Flip cake pan upside down and press into clay (like a cookie cutter), and remove excess clay. Confirm clay will fit inside cake pan, continuing to trim as needed.

Select flowers or greenery and lightly press into clay. Use brayer to roll flowers into clay (an extra set of hands is helpful to keep them in place initially). Remove flowers and use water to smooth out any cracks or uneven places.

Place clay in bottom of cake pan, and let dry overnight.

To Create Casting

Mix together plaster solution in bucket, following instructions provided on packaging (you'll want to wear gloves for this process!). Pour plaster into mold until it is 1 to 2 inches thick. Allow to dry for amount of time specified on plaster instructions. Once dry, remove plaster casting and mold from pan. Then separate casting from mold.

To Display

Get creative with how you want to display your artwork! You can feature it on a display stand or even lay a few small ones next to one another on a coffee table. If you made your mold in a picture frame, display your mold or casting in that same frame. Or if you want to skip the portion of the activity involving plaster, punch a small hole in the top of your clay mold before it dries to use as a hanging display or ornament.

WE TRUST HIS HOLY NAME

Psalms 30–34

DAY 9  WEEK 2

Psalm 30

Joy in the Morning

A PSALM; A DEDICATION SONG FOR THE HOUSE. OF DAVID.

1 I will exalt you, LORD,
because you have lifted me up
and have not allowed my enemies
to triumph over me.
2 LORD my God,
I cried to you for help, and you healed me.
3 LORD, you brought me up from Sheol;
you spared me from among those
going down to the Pit.

4 Sing to the LORD, you his faithful ones,
and praise his holy name.
5 For his anger lasts only a moment,
but his favor, a lifetime.
Weeping may stay overnight,
but there is joy in the morning.

6 When I was secure, I said,
"I will never be shaken."
7 LORD, when you showed your favor,
you made me stand like a strong mountain;
when you hid your face, I was terrified.
8 LORD, I called to you;
I sought favor from my Lord:
9 "What gain is there in my death,
if I go down to the Pit?
Will the dust praise you?
Will it proclaim your truth?
10 LORD, listen and be gracious to me;
LORD, be my helper."

11 You turned my lament into dancing;
you removed my sackcloth
and clothed me with gladness,
12 so that I can sing to you and not be silent.
LORD my God, I will praise you forever.

Psalm 31

A Plea for Protection

FOR THE CHOIR DIRECTOR. A PSALM OF DAVID.

1 LORD, I seek refuge in you;
let me never be disgraced.
Save me by your righteousness.
2 Listen closely to me; rescue me quickly.
Be a rock of refuge for me,
a mountain fortress to save me.
3 For you are my rock and my fortress;
you lead and guide me
for your name's sake.
4 You will free me from the net
that is secretly set for me,
for you are my refuge.
5 Into your hand I entrust my spirit;
you have redeemed me, LORD, God of truth.

6 I hate those who are devoted to worthless idols,
but I trust in the LORD.
7 I will rejoice and be glad in your faithful love
because you have seen my affliction.
You know the troubles of my soul
8 and have not handed me over to the enemy.
You have set my feet in a spacious place.

9 Be gracious to me, LORD,
because I am in distress;
my eyes are worn out from frustration—
my whole being as well.
10 Indeed, my life is consumed with grief
and my years with groaning;
my strength has failed
because of my iniquity,
and my bones waste away.
11 I am ridiculed by all my adversaries
and even by my neighbors.
I am dreaded by my acquaintances;
those who see me in the street run from me.

[12] I am forgotten: gone from memory
like a dead person—like broken pottery.
[13] I have heard the gossip of many;
terror is on every side.
When they conspired against me,
they plotted to take my life.

[14] But I trust in you, LORD;
I say, "You are my God."
[15] The course of my life is in your power;
rescue me from the power of my enemies
and from my persecutors.
[16] Make your face shine on your servant;
save me by your faithful love.
[17] LORD, do not let me be disgraced when I call on you.
Let the wicked be disgraced;
let them be quiet in Sheol.
[18] Let lying lips
that arrogantly speak against the righteous
in proud contempt be silenced.

[19] How great is your goodness,
which you have stored up for those who fear you.
In the presence of everyone you have acted
for those who take refuge in you.
[20] You hide them in the protection of your presence;
you conceal them in a shelter
from human schemes,
from quarrelsome tongues.
[21] Blessed be the LORD,
for he has wondrously shown his faithful love to me
in a city under siege.
[22] In my alarm I said,
"I am cut off from your sight."
But you heard the sound of my pleading
when I cried to you for help.

[23] Love the LORD, all his faithful ones.
The LORD protects the loyal,
but fully repays the arrogant.
[24] Be strong, and let your heart be courageous,
all you who put your hope in the LORD.

Psalm 32

The Joy of Forgiveness
OF DAVID. A *MASKIL.*

[1] How joyful is the one
whose transgression is forgiven,
whose sin is covered!
[2] How joyful is a person whom
the LORD does not charge with iniquity
and in whose spirit is no deceit!

[3] When I kept silent, my bones became brittle
from my groaning all day long.
[4] For day and night your hand was heavy on me;
my strength was drained
as in the summer's heat. *Selah*
[5] Then I acknowledged my sin to you
and did not conceal my iniquity.
I said, "I will confess my transgressions to the LORD,"
and you forgave the guilt of my sin. *Selah*

[6] Therefore let everyone who is faithful pray to
you immediately.
When great floodwaters come,
they will not reach him.
[7] You are my hiding place;
you protect me from trouble.
You surround me with joyful shouts of deliverance. *Selah*

[8] I will instruct you and show you the way to go;
with my eye on you, I will give counsel.
[9] Do not be like a horse or mule,
without understanding,
that must be controlled with bit and bridle
or else it will not come near you.

[10] Many pains come to the wicked,
but the one who trusts in the LORD
will have faithful love surrounding him.
[11] Be glad in the LORD and rejoice,
you righteous ones;
shout for joy,
all you upright in heart.

Psalm 33

Praise to the Creator

1 Rejoice in the Lord, you righteous ones;
praise from the upright is beautiful.
2 Praise the Lord with the lyre;
make music to him with a ten-stringed harp.
3 Sing a new song to him;
play skillfully on the strings, with a joyful shout.

4 For the word of the Lord is right,
and all his work is trustworthy.
5 He loves righteousness and justice;
the earth is full of the Lord's unfailing love.

6 The heavens were made by the word of the Lord,
and all the stars, by the breath of his mouth.
7 He gathers the water of the sea into a heap;
he puts the depths into storehouses.
8 Let the whole earth fear the Lord;
let all the inhabitants of the world stand in awe of him.
9 For he spoke, and it came into being;
he commanded, and it came into existence.

10 The Lord frustrates the counsel of the nations;
he thwarts the plans of the peoples.
11 The counsel of the Lord stands forever,
the plans of his heart from generation to generation.
12 Happy is the nation whose God is the Lord—
the people he has chosen to be his own possession!

13 The Lord looks down from heaven;
he observes everyone.
14 He gazes on all the inhabitants of the earth
from his dwelling place.
15 He forms the hearts of them all;
he considers all their works.
16 A king is not saved by a large army;
a warrior will not be rescued by great strength.
17 The horse is a false hope for safety;
it provides no escape by its great power.

18 But look, the Lord keeps his eye on those who fear him—
those who depend on his faithful love

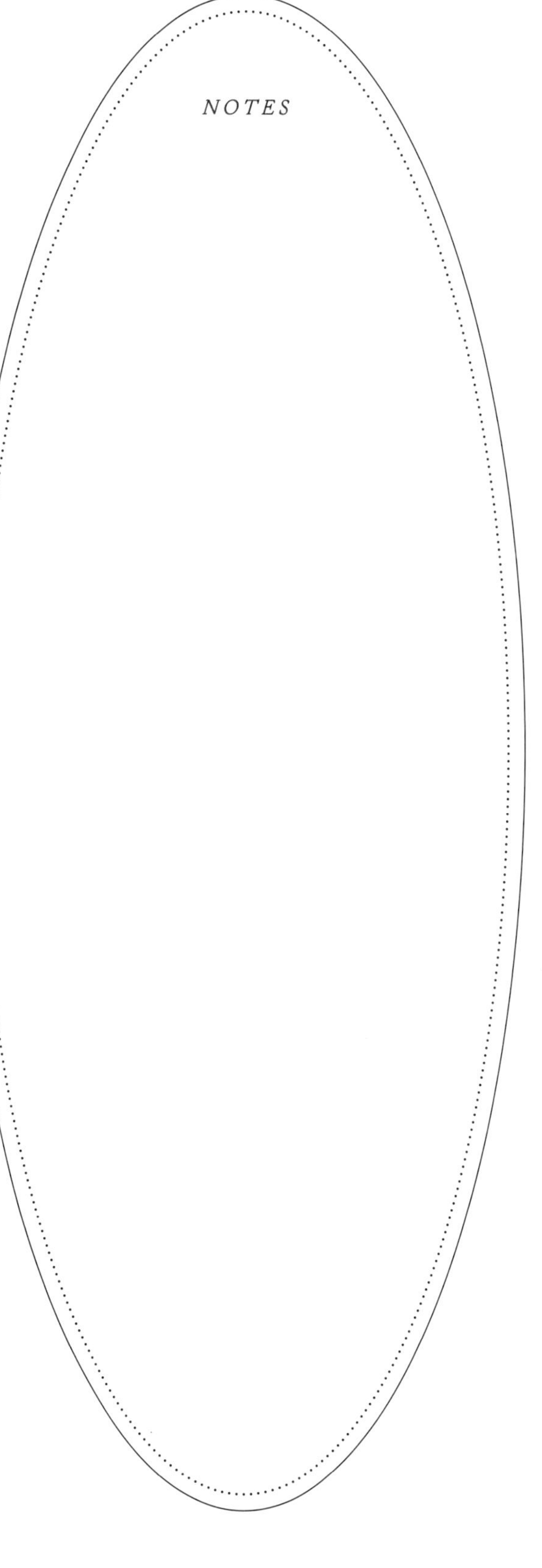

19 to rescue them from death
and to keep them alive in famine.

20 We wait for the LORD;
he is our help and shield.
21 For our hearts rejoice in him
because we trust in his holy name.
22 May your faithful love rest on us, LORD,
for we put our hope in you.

Psalm 34

The Lord Delivers the Righteous

CONCERNING DAVID, WHEN HE PRETENDED TO BE INSANE IN THE PRESENCE OF ABIMELECH, WHO DROVE HIM OUT, AND HE DEPARTED.

1 I will bless the LORD at all times;
his praise will always be on my lips.
2 I will boast in the LORD;
the humble will hear and be glad.
3 Proclaim the LORD's greatness with me;
let us exalt his name together.

4 I sought the LORD, and he answered me
and rescued me from all my fears.

5 THOSE WHO LOOK TO HIM ARE
RADIANT WITH JOY;
THEIR FACES WILL NEVER
BE ASHAMED.

6 This poor man cried, and the LORD heard him
and saved him from all his troubles.
7 The angel of the LORD encamps
around those who fear him, and rescues them.
8 Taste and see that the LORD is good.
How happy is the person who takes refuge in him!
9 You who are his holy ones, fear the LORD,
for those who fear him lack nothing.
10 Young lions lack food and go hungry,
but those who seek the LORD
will not lack any good thing.

11 Come, children, listen to me;
I will teach you the fear of the LORD.
12 Who is someone who desires life,
loving a long life to enjoy what is good?
13 Keep your tongue from evil
and your lips from deceitful speech.
14 Turn away from evil and do what is good;
seek peace and pursue it.

15 The eyes of the LORD are on the righteous,
and his ears are open to their cry for help.
16 The face of the LORD is set
against those who do what is evil,
to remove all memory of them from the earth.
17 The righteous cry out, and the LORD hears,
and rescues them from all their troubles.
18 The LORD is near the brokenhearted;
he saves those crushed in spirit.

19 One who is righteous has many adversities,
but the LORD rescues him from them all.
20 He protects all his bones;
not one of them is broken.
21 Evil brings death to the wicked,
and those who hate the righteous will be punished.
22 The LORD redeems the life of his servants,
and all who take refuge in him will not be punished.

Daily Response

Date:

WHAT ATTRIBUTES *of* GOD STOOD OUT TO ME?

HOW DO I CONNECT *with* THE HUMAN EXPERIENCES EXPRESSED *in* TODAY'S PSALMS?

Contextual markers

Poetic devices or patterns

Words or phrases for further study

HOW DO TODAY'S PSALMS GUIDE ME *in the* PRACTICES *of* LENT?

WHAT'S A VERSE *that* I WILL MEDITATE *on* TODAY?

DAY 10

Psalms 35–37

The LORD HELPS *and* DELIVERS

Psalm 35

Prayer for Victory

OF DAVID.

1 Oppose my opponents, LORD;
fight those who fight me.
2 Take your shields—large and small—
and come to my aid.
3 Draw the spear and javelin against my pursuers,
and assure me, "I am your deliverance."

4 Let those who intend to take my life
be disgraced and humiliated;
let those who plan to harm me
be turned back and ashamed.
5 Let them be like chaff in the wind,
with the angel of the LORD driving them away.
6 Let their way be dark and slippery,
with the angel of the LORD pursuing them.
7 They hid their net for me without cause;
they dug a pit for me without cause.
8 Let ruin come on him unexpectedly,
and let the net that he hid ensnare him;
let him fall into it—to his ruin.

9 Then I will rejoice in the LORD;
I will delight in his deliverance.
10 All my bones will say,
"LORD, who is like you,
rescuing the poor from one too strong for him,
the poor or the needy from one who robs him?"

11 Malicious witnesses come forward;
they question me about things I do not know.
12 They repay me evil for good,
making me desolate.
13 Yet when they were sick,
my clothing was sackcloth;
I humbled myself with fasting,
and my prayer was genuine.
14 I went about mourning as if for my friend or brother;
I was bowed down with grief,
like one mourning for a mother.
15 But when I stumbled, they gathered in glee;
they gathered against me.

Assailants I did not know
tore at me and did not stop.
16 With godless mockery
they gnashed their teeth at me.

17 Lord, how long will you look on?
Rescue me from their ravages;
rescue my precious life from the young lions.
18 I will praise you in the great assembly;
I will exalt you among many people.
19 Do not let my deceitful enemies rejoice over me;
do not let those who hate me without cause
wink at me maliciously.
20 For they do not speak in friendly ways,
but contrive fraudulent schemes
against those who live peacefully in the land.
21 They open their mouths wide against me and say,
"Aha, aha! We saw it!"

22 You saw it, LORD; do not be silent.
Lord, do not be far from me.
23 Wake up and rise to my defense,
to my cause, my God and my Lord!
24 Vindicate me, LORD my God,
in keeping with your righteousness,
and do not let them rejoice over me.
25 Do not let them say in their hearts,
"Aha! Just what we wanted."
Do not let them say,
"We have swallowed him up!"
26 Let those who rejoice at my misfortune
be disgraced and humiliated;
let those who exalt themselves over me
be clothed with shame and reproach.

27 Let those who want my vindication
shout for joy and be glad;
let them continually say,
"The LORD be exalted.
He takes pleasure in his servant's well-being."
28 And my tongue will proclaim your righteousness,
your praise all day long.

Psalm 36

Human Wickedness and God's Love

FOR THE CHOIR DIRECTOR. OF DAVID, THE LORD'S SERVANT.

1 An oracle within my heart
concerning the transgression of the wicked person:
Dread of God has no effect on him.
2 For with his flattering opinion of himself,
he does not discover and hate his iniquity.
3 The words from his mouth are malicious and deceptive;
he has stopped acting wisely and doing good.
4 Even on his bed he makes malicious plans.
He sets himself on a path that is not good,
and he does not reject evil.

5 LORD, your faithful love reaches to heaven,
your faithfulness to the clouds.
6 Your righteousness is like the highest mountains,
your judgments like the deepest sea.
LORD, you preserve people and animals.
7 How priceless your faithful love is, God!
People take refuge in the shadow of your wings.
8 They are filled from the abundance of your house.
You let them drink from your refreshing stream.
9 For the wellspring of life is with you.
By means of your light we see light.

10 Spread your faithful love over those who know you,
and your righteousness over the upright in heart.
11 Do not let the foot of the arrogant come near me
or the hand of the wicked drive me away.
12 There! The evildoers have fallen.
They have been thrown down and cannot rise.

Psalm 37

Instruction in Wisdom

OF DAVID.

1 Do not be agitated by evildoers;
do not envy those who do wrong.
2 For they wither quickly like grass
and wilt like tender green plants.

NOTES

3 Trust in the LORD and do what is good;
dwell in the land and live securely.
4 Take delight in the LORD,
and he will give you your heart's desires.

5 Commit your way to the LORD;
trust in him, and he will act,
6 making your righteousness shine like the dawn,
your justice like the noonday.

7 Be silent before the LORD and wait expectantly for him;
do not be agitated by one who prospers in his way,
by the person who carries out evil plans.

8 Refrain from anger and give up your rage;
do not be agitated—it can only bring harm.
9 For evildoers will be destroyed,
but those who put their hope in the LORD
will inherit the land.

10 A little while, and the wicked person will be no more;
though you look for him, he will not be there.
11 But the humble will inherit the land
and will enjoy abundant prosperity.

12 The wicked person schemes against the righteous
and gnashes his teeth at him.
13 The Lord laughs at him
because he sees that his day is coming.

14 The wicked have drawn the sword and strung the bow
to bring down the poor and needy
and to slaughter those whose way is upright.
15 Their swords will enter their own hearts,
and their bows will be broken.

16 The little that the righteous person has is better
than the abundance of many wicked people.
17 For the arms of the wicked will be broken,
but the LORD supports the righteous.

18 The LORD watches over the blameless all their days,
and their inheritance will last forever.
19 They will not be disgraced in times of adversity;
they will be satisfied in days of hunger.

20 But the wicked will perish;
the LORD's enemies, like the glory of the pastures,
will fade away—
they will fade away like smoke.

21 The wicked person borrows and does not repay,
but the righteous one is gracious and giving.
22 Those who are blessed by the LORD will inherit the land,
but those cursed by him will be destroyed.

23 A PERSON'S STEPS ARE
ESTABLISHED BY THE LORD,
AND HE TAKES PLEASURE
IN HIS WAY.
24 THOUGH HE FALLS, HE WILL
NOT BE OVERWHELMED,
BECAUSE THE LORD SUPPORTS
HIM WITH HIS HAND.

25 I have been young and now I am old,
yet I have not seen the righteous abandoned
or his children begging for bread.
26 He is always generous, always lending,
and his children are a blessing.

27 Turn away from evil, do what is good,
and settle permanently.
28 For the LORD loves justice
and will not abandon his faithful ones.
They are kept safe forever,
but the children of the wicked will be destroyed.
29 The righteous will inherit the land
and dwell in it permanently.

30 The mouth of the righteous utters wisdom;
his tongue speaks what is just.
31 The instruction of his God is in his heart;
his steps do not falter.

32 The wicked one lies in wait for the righteous
and intends to kill him;
33 the LORD will not leave him
in the power of the wicked one
or allow him to be condemned when he is judged.

34 Wait for the LORD and keep his way,
and he will exalt you to inherit the land.
You will watch when the wicked are destroyed.

35 I have seen a wicked, violent person
well-rooted, like a flourishing native tree.
36 Then I passed by and noticed he was gone;
I searched for him, but he could not be found.

37 Watch the blameless and observe the upright,
for the person of peace will have a future.
38 But transgressors will all be eliminated;
the future of the wicked will be destroyed.

39 The salvation of the righteous is from the LORD,
their refuge in a time of distress.
40 The LORD helps and delivers them;
he will deliver them from the wicked and will save them
because they take refuge in him.

Daily Response

Date:

WHAT ATTRIBUTES *of* GOD STOOD OUT TO ME?

HOW DO I CONNECT *with* THE HUMAN EXPERIENCES EXPRESSED *in* TODAY'S PSALMS?

Contextual markers

Poetic devices or patterns

Words or phrases for further study

HOW DO TODAY'S PSALMS GUIDE ME *in the* PRACTICES *of* LENT?

WHAT'S A VERSE *that* I WILL MEDITATE *on* TODAY?

PSALMS 38–41

DAY 11

WEEK 2

HURRY *to* HELP ME, MY LORD

Psalm 38

Prayer of a Suffering Sinner

A PSALM OF DAVID TO BRING REMEMBRANCE.

1 LORD, do not punish me in your anger
or discipline me in your wrath.
2 For your arrows have sunk into me,
and your hand has pressed down on me.

3 There is no soundness in my body
because of your indignation;
there is no health in my bones
because of my sin.
4 For my iniquities have flooded over my head;
they are a burden too heavy for me to bear.
5 My wounds are foul and festering
because of my foolishness.
6 I am bent over and brought very low;
all day long I go around in mourning.
7 For my insides are full of burning pain,
and there is no soundness in my body.
8 I am faint and severely crushed;
I groan because of the anguish of my heart.

9 Lord, my every desire is in front of you;
my sighing is not hidden from you.
10 My heart races, my strength leaves me,
and even the light of my eyes has faded.
11 My loved ones and friends stand back from my affliction,
and my relatives stand at a distance.
12 Those who intend to kill me set traps,
and those who want to harm me threaten to destroy me;
they plot treachery all day long.

13 I am like a deaf person; I do not hear.
I am like a speechless person
who does not open his mouth.
14 I am like a man who does not hear
and has no arguments in his mouth.
15 For I put my hope in you, LORD;
you will answer me, my Lord, my God.
16 For I said, "Don't let them rejoice over me—
those who are arrogant toward me when I stumble."
17 For I am about to fall,
and my pain is constantly with me.
18 So I confess my iniquity;
I am anxious because of my sin.
19 But my enemies are vigorous and powerful;
many hate me for no reason.
20 Those who repay evil for good
attack me for pursuing good.

21 LORD, do not abandon me;
my God, do not be far from me.
22 Hurry to help me,
my Lord, my salvation.

Psalm 39

The Fleeting Nature of Life

FOR THE CHOIR DIRECTOR, FOR JEDUTHUN. A PSALM OF DAVID.

1 I said, "I will guard my ways
so that I may not sin with my tongue;
I will guard my mouth with a muzzle
as long as the wicked are in my presence."
2 I was speechless and quiet;
I kept silent, even from speaking good,
and my pain intensified.
3 My heart grew hot within me;
as I mused, a fire burned.
I spoke with my tongue:
4 "LORD, make me aware of my end
and the number of my days
so that I will know how short-lived I am.
5 In fact, you have made my days just inches long,
and my life span is as nothing to you.
Yes, every human being stands as only a vapor. *Selah*
6 Yes, a person goes about like a mere shadow.
Indeed, they rush around in vain,
gathering possessions
without knowing who will get them.

7 "Now, Lord, what do I wait for?
My hope is in you.
8 Rescue me from all my transgressions;
do not make me the taunt of fools.
9 I am speechless; I do not open my mouth
because of what you have done.
10 Remove your torment from me.
Because of the force of your hand I am finished.
11 You discipline a person with punishment for iniquity,
consuming like a moth what is precious to him;
yes, every human being is only a vapor. *Selah*

12 "Hear my prayer, LORD,
and listen to my cry for help;
do not be silent at my tears.
For I am here with you as an alien,
a temporary resident like all my ancestors.
13 Turn your angry gaze from me
so that I may be cheered up
before I die and am gone."

Psalm 40

Thanksgiving and a Cry for Help

FOR THE CHOIR DIRECTOR. A PSALM OF DAVID.

1 I WAITED PATIENTLY FOR THE LORD,
AND HE TURNED TO ME AND HEARD MY
CRY FOR HELP.

2 He brought me up from a desolate pit,
out of the muddy clay,
and set my feet on a rock,
making my steps secure.
3 He put a new song in my mouth,
a hymn of praise to our God.
Many will see and fear,
and they will trust in the LORD.

4 How happy is anyone
who has put his trust in the LORD
and has not turned to the proud
or to those who run after lies!
5 LORD my God, you have done many things—
your wondrous works and your plans for us;
none can compare with you.
If I were to report and speak of them,
they are more than can be told.

6 You do not delight in sacrifice and offering;
you open my ears to listen.
You do not ask for a whole burnt offering or a sin offering.
7 Then I said, "See, I have come;
in the scroll it is written about me.
8 I delight to do your will, my God,
and your instruction is deep within me."

9 I proclaim righteousness in the great assembly;
see, I do not keep my mouth closed—
as you know, LORD.
10 I did not hide your righteousness in my heart;
I spoke about your faithfulness and salvation;
I did not conceal your constant love and truth
from the great assembly.

11 LORD, you do not withhold your compassion from me.
Your constant love and truth will always guard me.

12 For troubles without number have surrounded me;
my iniquities have overtaken me; I am unable to see.
They are more than the hairs of my head,
and my courage leaves me.
13 Lord, be pleased to rescue me;
hurry to help me, Lord.

14 Let those who intend to take my life
be disgraced and confounded.
Let those who wish me harm
be turned back and humiliated.
15 Let those who say to me, "Aha, aha!"
be appalled because of their shame.

16 Let all who seek you rejoice and be glad in you;
let those who love your salvation continually say,
"The Lord is great!"
17 I am oppressed and needy;
may the Lord think of me.
You are my helper and my deliverer;
my God, do not delay.

Psalm 41

Victory in Spite of Betrayal

FOR THE CHOIR DIRECTOR. A PSALM OF DAVID.

1 Happy is one who is considerate of the poor;
the Lord will save him in a day of adversity.
2 The Lord will keep him and preserve him;
he will be blessed in the land.
You will not give him over to the desire of his enemies.
3 The Lord will sustain him on his sickbed;
you will heal him on the bed where he lies.

4 I said, "Lord, be gracious to me;
heal me, for I have sinned against you."
5 My enemies speak maliciously about me:
"When will he die and be forgotten?"
6 When one of them comes to visit, he speaks deceitfully;
he stores up evil in his heart;
he goes out and talks.
7 All who hate me whisper together about me;
they plan to harm me.
8 "Something awful has overwhelmed him,
and he won't rise again from where he lies!"
9 Even my friend in whom I trusted,
one who ate my bread,
has raised his heel against me.

10 But you, Lord, be gracious to me and raise me up;
then I will repay them.
11 By this I know that you delight in me:
my enemy does not shout in triumph over me.
12 You supported me because of my integrity
and set me in your presence forever.

13 Blessed be the Lord God of Israel,
from everlasting to everlasting.
Amen and amen.

Daily Response

Date:

WHAT ATTRIBUTES *of* GOD STOOD OUT TO ME?

HOW DO I CONNECT *with* THE HUMAN EXPERIENCES EXPRESSED *in* TODAY'S PSALMS?

Contextual markers

Poetic devices or patterns

Words or phrases for further study

HOW DO TODAY'S PSALMS GUIDE ME *in the* PRACTICES *of* LENT?

WHAT'S A VERSE *that* I WILL MEDITATE *on* TODAY?

I Will Still Praise Him

PSALMS 42–45

DAY 12 .... WEEK 2

Psalm 42

Longing for God

FOR THE CHOIR DIRECTOR. A *MASKIL* OF THE SONS OF KORAH.

1 As a deer longs for flowing streams,
so I long for you, God.
2 I thirst for God, the living God.
When can I come and appear before God?
3 My tears have been my food day and night,
while all day long people say to me,
"Where is your God?"
4 I remember this as I pour out my heart:
how I walked with many,
leading the festive procession to the house of God,
with joyful and thankful shouts.

5 Why, my soul, are you so dejected?
Why are you in such turmoil?
Put your hope in God, for I will still praise him,
my Savior and my God.
6 I am deeply depressed;
therefore I remember you from the land of Jordan
and the peaks of Hermon, from Mount Mizar.
7 Deep calls to deep in the roar of your waterfalls;
all your breakers and your billows have swept over me.
8 The Lord will send his faithful love by day;
his song will be with me in the night—
a prayer to the God of my life.

9 I will say to God, my rock,
"Why have you forgotten me?
Why must I go about in sorrow
because of the enemy's oppression?"
10 My adversaries taunt me,
as if crushing my bones,
while all day long they say to me,
"Where is your God?"
11 Why, my soul, are you so dejected?
Why are you in such turmoil?
Put your hope in God, for I will still praise him,
my Savior and my God.

Psalm 43

1 Vindicate me, God, and champion my cause
against an unfaithful nation;
rescue me from the deceitful and unjust person.
2 For you are the God of my refuge.
Why have you rejected me?
Why must I go about in sorrow
because of the enemy's oppression?

3 Send your light and your truth; let them lead me.
Let them bring me to your holy mountain,
to your dwelling place.
4 Then I will come to the altar of God,
to God, my greatest joy.
I will praise you with the lyre,
God, my God.

5 Why, my soul, are you so dejected?
Why are you in such turmoil?
Put your hope in God, for I will still praise him,
my Savior and my God.

NOTES

Psalm 44

Israel's Complaint

FOR THE CHOIR DIRECTOR. A *MASKIL* OF THE SONS OF KORAH.

1 God, we have heard with our ears—
our ancestors have told us—
the work you accomplished in their days,
in days long ago:
2 In order to plant them,
you displaced the nations by your hand;
in order to settle them,
you brought disaster on the peoples.
3 For they did not take the land by their sword—
their arm did not bring them victory—
but by your right hand, your arm,
and the light of your face,
because you were favorable toward them.

4 You are my King, my God,
who ordains victories for Jacob.
5 Through you we drive back our foes;
through your name we trample our enemies.
6 For I do not trust in my bow,
and my sword does not bring me victory.
7 But you give us victory over our foes
and let those who hate us be disgraced.
8 We boast in God all day long;
we will praise your name forever. *Selah*

9 But you have rejected and humiliated us;
you do not march out with our armies.
10 You make us retreat from the foe,
and those who hate us
have taken plunder for themselves.
11 You hand us over to be eaten like sheep
and scatter us among the nations.
12 You sell your people for nothing;
you make no profit from selling them.

13 You make us an object of reproach to our neighbors,
a source of mockery and ridicule to those around us.
14 You make us a joke among the nations,
a laughingstock among the peoples.
15 My disgrace is before me all day long,
and shame has covered my face,
16 because of the taunts of the scorner and reviler,
because of the enemy and avenger.

17 All this has happened to us,
but we have not forgotten you
or betrayed your covenant.
18 Our hearts have not turned back;
our steps have not strayed from your path.
19 But you have crushed us in a haunt of jackals
and have covered us with deepest darkness.
20 If we had forgotten the name of our God
and spread out our hands to a foreign god,
21 wouldn't God have found this out,
since he knows the secrets of the heart?
22 Because of you we are being put to death all day long;
we are counted as sheep to be slaughtered.

23 Wake up, Lord! Why are you sleeping?
Get up! Don't reject us forever!
24 Why do you hide
and forget our affliction and oppression?
25 For we have sunk down to the dust;
our bodies cling to the ground.
26 Rise up! Help us!
Redeem us because of your faithful love.

Psalm 45

A Royal Wedding Song

FOR THE CHOIR DIRECTOR: ACCORDING TO "THE LILIES."
A *MASKIL* OF THE SONS OF KORAH. A LOVE SONG.

1 My heart is moved by a noble theme
as I recite my verses to the king;
my tongue is the pen of a skillful writer.
2 You are the most handsome of men;
grace flows from your lips.
Therefore God has blessed you forever.

3 Mighty warrior, strap your sword at your side.
In your majesty and splendor—
4 in your splendor ride triumphantly
in the cause of truth, humility, and justice.
May your right hand show your awe-inspiring acts.
5 Your sharpened arrows pierce the hearts of the
king's enemies;
the peoples fall under you.

6 Your throne, God, is forever and ever;
the scepter of your kingdom is a scepter of justice.
7 You love righteousness and hate wickedness;
therefore God, your God, has anointed you with the oil of joy
more than your companions.
8 Myrrh, aloes, and cassia perfume all your garments;
from ivory palaces harps bring you joy.
9 Kings' daughters are among your honored women;
the queen, adorned with gold from Ophir,
stands at your right hand.

10 Listen, daughter, pay attention and consider:
Forget your people and your father's house,
11 and the king will desire your beauty.
Bow down to him, for he is your lord.
12 The daughter of Tyre, the wealthy people,
will seek your favor with gifts.

13 In her chamber, the royal daughter is all glorious,
her clothing embroidered with gold.
14 In colorful garments she is led to the king;
after her, the virgins, her companions, are brought to you.
15 They are led in with gladness and rejoicing;
they enter the king's palace.

16 Your sons will succeed your ancestors;
you will make them princes throughout the land.
17 I will cause your name to be remembered for all generations;
therefore the peoples will praise you forever and ever.

Daily Response

Date:

WHAT ATTRIBUTES *of* GOD STOOD OUT TO ME?

HOW DO I CONNECT *with* THE HUMAN EXPERIENCES EXPRESSED *in* TODAY'S PSALMS?

Contextual markers

Poetic devices or patterns

Words or phrases for further study

HOW DO TODAY'S PSALMS GUIDE ME *in the* PRACTICES *of* LENT?

WHAT'S A VERSE *that* I WILL MEDITATE *on* TODAY?

Week Two *Response*

Use Psalm 32 to respond in prayer, allowing the words of Scripture to guide your prayer. Talk to the Lord about whatever the psalm brings to mind. Refer back to the example on page 46 if you need to.

Psalm 32

The Joy of Forgiveness

OF DAVID. A *MASKIL.*

1 How joyful is the one
whose transgression is forgiven,
whose sin is covered!

2 How joyful is a person whom
the LORD does not charge with iniquity
and in whose spirit is no deceit!

3 When I kept silent, my bones became brittle
from my groaning all day long.

4 For day and night your hand was heavy on me;
my strength was drained
as in the summer's heat. *Selah*

5 Then I acknowledged my sin to you
and did not conceal my iniquity.
I said, "I will confess my transgressions to the LORD,"
and you forgave the guilt of my sin. *Selah*

6 Therefore let everyone who is faithful pray to
you immediately.
When great floodwaters come,
they will not reach him.

7 You are my hiding place;
you protect me from trouble.
You surround me with joyful shouts of deliverance.
Selah

8 I will instruct you and show you the way to go;
with my eye on you, I will give counsel.

9 Do not be like a horse or mule,
without understanding,
that must be controlled with bit and bridle
or else it will not come near you.

10 Many pains come to the wicked,
but the one who trusts in the LORD
will have faithful love surrounding him.

11 Be glad in the LORD and rejoice,
you righteous ones;
shout for joy,
all you upright in heart.

GRACE *Day*

TAKE EACH SATURDAY *to* CATCH UP ON YOUR READING, PRAY, *and* REST *in the* PRESENCE *of the* LORD *with* PASSAGES *from* SCRIPTURE THAT WE TRADITIONALLY READ DURING *the* LENTEN SEASON.

*Now if we died with Christ,
we believe that we will also live with
him, because we know that Christ,
having been raised from the dead, will
not die again. Death no longer rules
over him. For the death he died, he
died to sin once for all time; but the life
he lives, he lives to God. So, you too
consider yourselves dead to sin and
alive to God in Christ Jesus.*

ROMANS 6:8–11

DAY 14 - WEEK 2

WEEKLY TRUTH

SCRIPTURE IS GOD BREATHED *and* TRUE. WHEN WE MEMORIZE IT, WE CARRY HIS WORD *with* US WHEREVER WE GO.

EACH SUNDAY DURING THIS PLAN, WE ARE READING *a* DIFFERENT HALLEL PSALM *(turn back to page 50 if you need a reminder about the significance of Hallel psalms)* *and* MEMORIZING ONE *of* ITS VERSES.

THIS WEEK, MEMORIZE PSALM 114:7 AS YOU MEDITATE *on the* PSALM *as a* WHOLE.

Psalm 114

God's Deliverance of Israel

1 When Israel came out of Egypt—
the house of Jacob from a people
who spoke a foreign language—
2 Judah became his sanctuary,
Israel, his dominion.

3 The sea looked and fled;
the Jordan turned back.
4 The mountains skipped like rams,
the hills, like lambs.
5 Why was it, sea, that you fled?
Jordan, that you turned back?
6 Mountains, that you skipped like rams?
Hills, like lambs?

7 Tremble, earth, at the presence of the Lord,
at the presence of the God of Jacob,
8 who turned the rock into a pool,
the flint into a spring.

SEE TIPS FOR MEMORIZING SCRIPTURE ON PAGE 272.

GOD WILL REDEEM ME

Psalms 46–49

DAY 15  WEEK 3

Psalm 46

God Our Refuge

FOR THE CHOIR DIRECTOR. A SONG OF THE SONS OF KORAH. ACCORDING TO *ALAMOTH.*

1 God is our refuge and strength,
a helper who is always found
in times of trouble.
2 Therefore we will not be afraid,
though the earth trembles
and the mountains topple
into the depths of the seas,
3 though its water roars and foams
and the mountains quake with its turmoil. *Selah*

4 There is a river—
its streams delight the city of God,
the holy dwelling place of the Most High.
5 God is within her; she will not be toppled.
God will help her when the morning dawns.
6 Nations rage, kingdoms topple;
the earth melts when he lifts his voice.
7 The Lord of Armies is with us;
the God of Jacob is our stronghold. *Selah*

8 Come, see the works of the Lord,
who brings devastation on the earth.
9 He makes wars cease throughout the earth.
He shatters bows and cuts spears to pieces;
he sets wagons ablaze.
10 "Stop fighting, and know that I am God,
exalted among the nations, exalted on the earth."
11 The Lord of Armies is with us;
the God of Jacob is our stronghold. *Selah*

Psalm 47

God Our King

FOR THE CHOIR DIRECTOR. A PSALM OF THE SONS OF KORAH.

1 Clap your hands, all you peoples;
shout to God with a jubilant cry.
2 For the Lord, the Most High, is awe-inspiring,
a great King over the whole earth.
3 He subdues peoples under us
and nations under our feet.
4 He chooses for us our inheritance—
the pride of Jacob, whom he loves. *Selah*

5 God ascends among shouts of joy,
the Lord, with the sound of a ram's horn.
6 Sing praise to God, sing praise;
sing praise to our King, sing praise!
7 Sing a song of wisdom,
for God is King of the whole earth.

8 God reigns over the nations;
God is seated on his holy throne.
9 The nobles of the peoples have assembled
with the people of the God of Abraham.
For the leaders of the earth belong to God;
he is greatly exalted.

Psalm 48

Zion Exalted

A SONG. A PSALM OF THE SONS OF KORAH.

1 The Lord is great and highly praised
in the city of our God.
His holy mountain, 2 rising splendidly,
is the joy of the whole earth.
Mount Zion—the summit of Zaphon—
is the city of the great King.
3 God is known as a stronghold
in its citadels.

4 Look! The kings assembled;
they advanced together.
5 They looked and froze with fear;
they fled in terror.
6 Trembling seized them there,
agony like that of a woman in labor,
7 as you wrecked the ships of Tarshish
with the east wind.

[8] Just as we heard, so we have seen
in the city of the Lord of Armies,
in the city of our God;
God will establish it forever. *Selah*

[9] GOD, WITHIN YOUR TEMPLE,
WE CONTEMPLATE YOUR
FAITHFUL LOVE.

[10] Like your name, God, so your praise
reaches to the ends of the earth;
your right hand is filled with justice.
[11] Mount Zion is glad.
Judah's villages rejoice
because of your judgments.

[12] Go around Zion, encircle it;
count its towers,
[13] note its ramparts; tour its citadels
so that you can tell a future generation:
[14] "This God, our God forever and ever—
he will always lead us."

Psalm 49

Misplaced Trust in Wealth

FOR THE CHOIR DIRECTOR. A PSALM OF THE SONS OF KORAH.

[1] Hear this, all you peoples;
listen, all who inhabit the world,
[2] both low and high,
rich and poor together.
[3] My mouth speaks wisdom;
my heart's meditation brings understanding.
[4] I turn my ear to a proverb;
I explain my riddle with a lyre.

[5] Why should I fear in times of trouble?
The iniquity of my foes surrounds me.
[6] They trust in their wealth
and boast of their abundant riches.
[7] Yet these cannot redeem a person
or pay his ransom to God—
[8] since the price of redeeming him is too costly,
one should forever stop trying—
[9] so that he may live forever
and not see the Pit.

[10] For one can see that the wise die;
the foolish and stupid also pass away.
Then they leave their wealth to others.
[11] Their graves are their permanent homes,
their dwellings from generation to generation,
though they have named estates after themselves.
[12] But despite his assets, mankind will not last;
he is like the animals that perish.

[13] This is the way of those who are arrogant,
and of their followers,
who approve of their words. *Selah*
[14] Like sheep they are headed for Sheol;
Death will shepherd them.
The upright will rule over them in the morning,
and their form will waste away in Sheol,
far from their lofty abode.
[15] But God will redeem me
from the power of Sheol,
for he will take me. *Selah*

[16] Do not be afraid when a person gets rich,
when the wealth of his house increases.
[17] For when he dies, he will take nothing at all;
his wealth will not follow him down.
[18] Though he blesses himself during his lifetime—
and you are acclaimed when you do well for yourself—
[19] he will go to the generation of his ancestors;
they will never see the light.
[20] Mankind, with his assets
but without understanding,
is like the animals that perish.

Daily Response

Date:

WHAT ATTRIBUTES *of* GOD STOOD OUT TO ME?

HOW DO I CONNECT *with* THE HUMAN EXPERIENCES EXPRESSED *in* TODAY'S PSALMS?

Contextual markers

Poetic devices or patterns

Words or phrases for further study

HOW DO TODAY'S PSALMS GUIDE ME *in the* PRACTICES *of* LENT?

WHAT'S A VERSE *that* I WILL MEDITATE *on* TODAY?

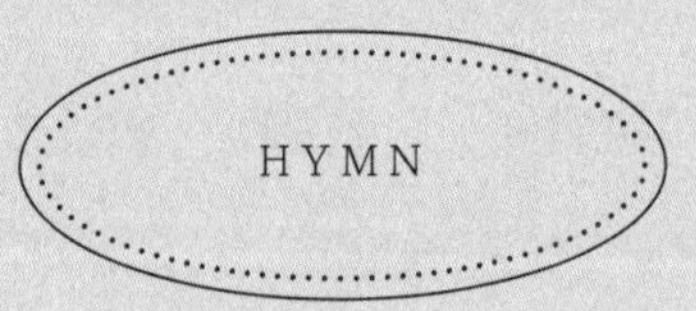

WHAT WONDROUS LOVE IS THIS

WORDS

American Folk Hymn

MUSIC

William Walker's Southern Harmony; arrangement by William J. Reynolds

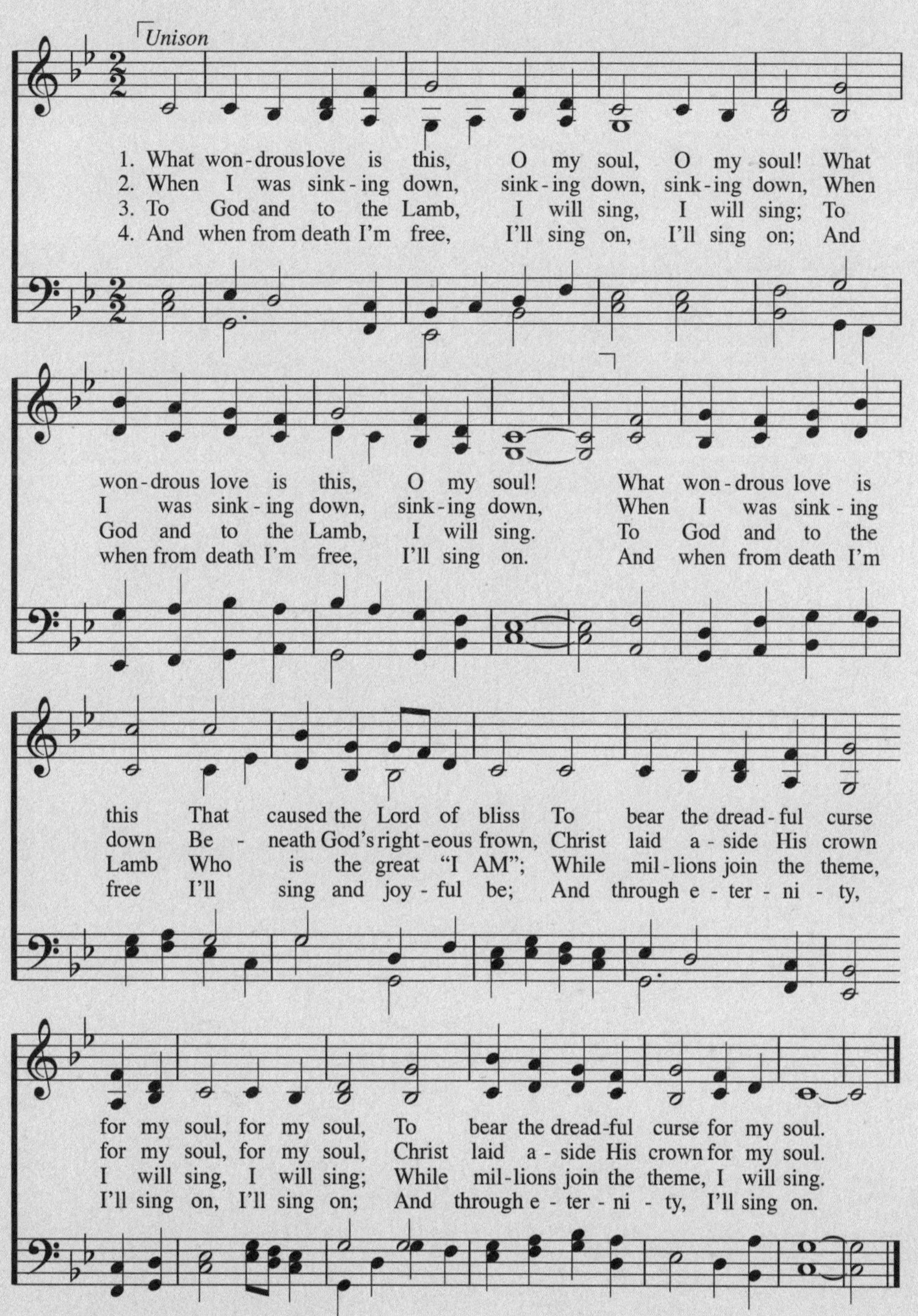
Unison
1. What won-drous love is this, O my soul, O my soul! What
2. When I was sink-ing down, sink-ing down, sink-ing down, When
3. To God and to the Lamb, I will sing, I will sing; To
4. And when from death I'm free, I'll sing on, I'll sing on; And
won-drous love is this, O my soul! What won-drous love is
I was sink-ing down, sink-ing down, When I was sink-ing
God and to the Lamb, I will sing. To God and to the
when from death I'm free, I'll sing on. And when from death I'm
this That caused the Lord of bliss To bear the dread-ful curse
down Be-neath God's right-eous frown, Christ laid a-side His crown
Lamb Who is the great "I AM"; While mil-lions join the theme,
free I'll sing and joy-ful be; And through e-ter-ni-ty,
for my soul, for my soul, To bear the dread-ful curse for my soul.
for my soul, for my soul, Christ laid a-side His crown for my soul.
I will sing, I will sing; While mil-lions join the theme, I will sing.
I'll sing on, I'll sing on; And through e-ter-ni-ty, I'll sing on.

BE GRACIOUS TO ME, GOD

Psalms 50–54

BE GRACIOUS *to* ME, GOD,
ACCORDING *to* YOUR FAITHFUL
LOVE; ACCORDING *to* YOUR
ABUNDANT COMPASSION,
BLOT OUT MY REBELLION.

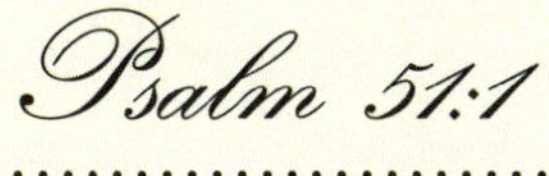

DAY
16

WEEK
3

Psalm 50

God as Judge

A PSALM OF ASAPH.

1 The Mighty One, God, the LORD, speaks;
he summons the earth
from the rising of the sun to its setting.
2 From Zion, the perfection of beauty,
God appears in radiance.
3 Our God is coming; he will not be silent!
Devouring fire precedes him,
and a storm rages around him.
4 On high, he summons heaven and earth
in order to judge his people:
5 "Gather my faithful ones to me,
those who made a covenant with me by sacrifice."
6 The heavens proclaim his righteousness,
for God is the Judge. *Selah*

7 "Listen, my people, and I will speak;
I will testify against you, Israel.
I am God, your God.
8 I do not rebuke you for your sacrifices
or for your burnt offerings,
which are continually before me.
9 I will not take a bull from your household
or male goats from your pens,
10 for every animal of the forest is mine,
the cattle on a thousand hills.
11 I know every bird of the mountains,
and the creatures of the field are mine.
12 If I were hungry, I would not tell you,
for the world and everything in it is mine.
13 Do I eat the flesh of bulls
or drink the blood of goats?
14 Offer a thanksgiving sacrifice to God,
and pay your vows to the Most High.
15 Call on me in a day of trouble;
I will rescue you, and you will honor me."

16 But God says to the wicked:
"What right do you have to recite my statutes
and to take my covenant on your lips?
17 You hate instruction
and fling my words behind you.
18 When you see a thief,
you make friends with him,
and you associate with adulterers.
19 You unleash your mouth for evil
and harness your tongue for deceit.
20 You sit, maligning your brother,
slandering your mother's son.
21 You have done these things, and I kept silent;
you thought I was just like you.
But I will rebuke you
and lay out the case before you.

22 "Understand this, you who forget God,
or I will tear you apart,
and there will be no one to rescue you.
23 Whoever offers a thanksgiving sacrifice honors me,
and whoever orders his conduct,
I will show him the salvation of God."

Psalm 51

A Prayer for Restoration

FOR THE CHOIR DIRECTOR. A PSALM OF DAVID, WHEN THE PROPHET NATHAN CAME TO HIM AFTER HE HAD GONE TO BATHSHEBA.

1 Be gracious to me, God,
according to your faithful love;
according to your abundant compassion,
blot out my rebellion.
2 Completely wash away my guilt
and cleanse me from my sin.
3 For I am conscious of my rebellion,
and my sin is always before me.
4 Against you—you alone—I have sinned
and done this evil in your sight.
So you are right when you pass sentence;
you are blameless when you judge.
5 Indeed, I was guilty when I was born;
I was sinful when my mother conceived me.

6 Surely you desire integrity in the inner self,
and you teach me wisdom deep within.
7 Purify me with hyssop, and I will be clean;
wash me, and I will be whiter than snow.
8 Let me hear joy and gladness;
let the bones you have crushed rejoice.
9 Turn your face away from my sins
and blot out all my guilt.

10 God, create a clean heart for me
and renew a steadfast spirit within me.
11 Do not banish me from your presence
or take your Holy Spirit from me.
12 Restore the joy of your salvation to me,
and sustain me by giving me a willing spirit.
13 Then I will teach the rebellious your ways,
and sinners will return to you.

14 Save me from the guilt of bloodshed, God—
God of my salvation—
and my tongue will sing of your righteousness.
15 Lord, open my lips,
and my mouth will declare your praise.
16 You do not want a sacrifice, or I would give it;
you are not pleased with a burnt offering.
17 The sacrifice pleasing to God is a broken spirit.
You will not despise a broken and humbled heart, God.

18 In your good pleasure, cause Zion to prosper;
build the walls of Jerusalem.
19 Then you will delight in righteous sacrifices,
whole burnt offerings;
then bulls will be offered on your altar.

Psalm 52

God Judges the Proud

FOR THE CHOIR DIRECTOR. A *MASKIL* OF DAVID. WHEN DOEG THE EDOMITE WENT AND REPORTED TO SAUL, TELLING HIM, "DAVID WENT TO AHIMELECH'S HOUSE."

1 Why boast about evil, you hero!
God's faithful love is constant.
2 Like a sharpened razor,

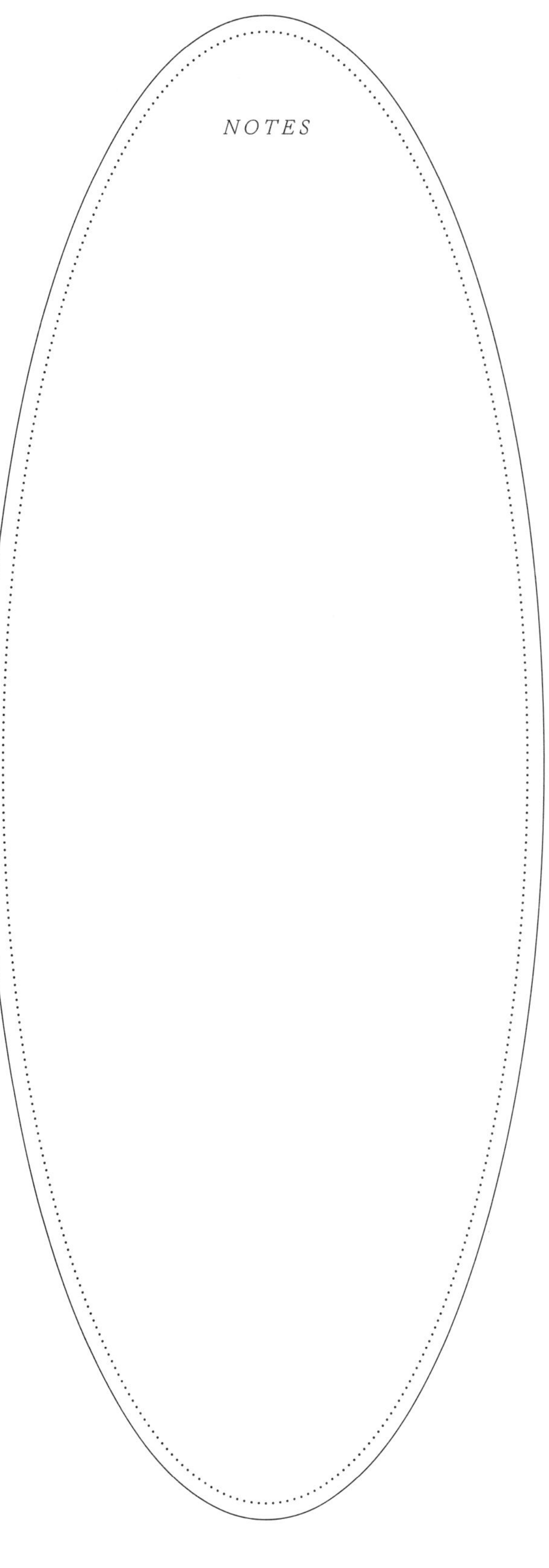

your tongue devises destruction,
working treachery.
3 You love evil instead of good,
lying instead of speaking truthfully. *Selah*
4 You love any words that destroy,
you treacherous tongue!

5 This is why God will bring you down forever.
He will take you, ripping you out of your tent;
he will uproot you from the land of the living. *Selah*
6 The righteous will see and fear,
and they will derisively say about that hero,
7 "Here is the man
who would not make God his refuge,
but trusted in the abundance of his riches,
taking refuge in his destructive behavior."

8 But I am like a flourishing olive tree
in the house of God;
I trust in God's faithful love forever and ever.
9 I will praise you forever for what you have done.
In the presence of your faithful people,
I will put my hope in your name, for it is good.

Psalm 53

A Portrait of Sinners

FOR THE CHOIR DIRECTOR: ON *MAHALATH*. A *MASKIL* OF DAVID.

1 The fool says in his heart, "There's no God."
They are corrupt, and they do vile deeds.
There is no one who does good.
2 God looks down from heaven on the human race
to see if there is one who is wise,
one who seeks God.
3 All have turned away;
all alike have become corrupt.
There is no one who does good,
not even one.

4 Will evildoers never understand?
They consume my people as they consume bread;
they do not call on God.
5 Then they will be filled with dread—
dread like no other—
because God will scatter
the bones of those who besiege you.
You will put them to shame,
for God has rejected them.

6 Oh, that Israel's deliverance would come from Zion!
When God restores the fortunes of his people,
let Jacob rejoice, let Israel be glad.

Psalm 54

Prayer for Deliverance

FOR THE CHOIR DIRECTOR: WITH STRINGED INSTRUMENTS. A *MASKIL* OF DAVID. WHEN THE ZIPHITES WENT AND SAID TO SAUL, "IS DAVID NOT HIDING AMONG US?"

1 God, save me by your name,
and vindicate me by your might!
2 God, hear my prayer;
listen to the words from my mouth.
3 For strangers rise up against me,
and violent men intend to kill me.
They do not let God guide them. *Selah*

4 God is my helper;
the Lord is the sustainer of my life.
5 He will repay my adversaries for their evil.
Because of your faithfulness, annihilate them.

6 I will sacrifice a freewill offering to you.
I will praise your name, LORD,
because it is good.
7 For he has rescued me from every trouble,
and my eye has looked down on my enemies.

Daily Response

Date:

WHAT ATTRIBUTES *of* GOD STOOD OUT TO ME?

HOW DO I CONNECT *with* THE HUMAN EXPERIENCES EXPRESSED *in* TODAY'S PSALMS?

Contextual markers

Poetic devices or patterns

Words or phrases for further study

HOW DO TODAY'S PSALMS GUIDE ME *in the* PRACTICES *of* LENT?

WHAT'S A VERSE *that* I WILL MEDITATE *on* TODAY?

I Call to God Most High

PSALMS 55–58

✿ ✿ ✿

DAY 17 ··················· WEEK 3

Psalm 55

Betrayal by a Friend

FOR THE CHOIR DIRECTOR: WITH STRINGED INSTRUMENTS.
A *MASKIL* OF DAVID.

1 God, listen to my prayer
and do not hide from my plea for help.
2 Pay attention to me and answer me.
I am restless and in turmoil with my complaint,
3 because of the enemy's words,
because of the pressure of the wicked.
For they bring down disaster on me
and harass me in anger.

4 My heart shudders within me;
terrors of death sweep over me.
5 Fear and trembling grip me;
horror has overwhelmed me.
6 I said, "If only I had wings like a dove!
I would fly away and find rest.
7 How far away I would flee;
I would stay in the wilderness. *Selah*
8 I would hurry to my shelter
from the raging wind and the storm."

9 Lord, confuse and confound their speech,
for I see violence and strife in the city;
10 day and night they make the rounds on its walls.
Crime and trouble are within it;
11 destruction is inside it;
oppression and deceit never leave its marketplace.

12 Now it is not an enemy who insults me—
otherwise I could bear it;
it is not a foe who rises up against me—
otherwise I could hide from him.
13 But it is you, a man who is my peer,
my companion and good friend!
14 We used to have close fellowship;
we walked with the crowd into the house of God.

15 Let death take them by surprise;
let them go down to Sheol alive,
because evil is in their homes and within them.
16 But I call to God,
and the Lord will save me.
17 I complain and groan morning, noon, and night,
and he hears my voice.
18 Though many are against me,
he will redeem me from my battle unharmed.
19 God, the one enthroned from long ago,
will hear and will humiliate them *Selah*
because they do not change
and do not fear God.

20 My friend acts violently
against those at peace with him;
he violates his covenant.

[21] His buttery words are smooth,
but war is in his heart.
His words are softer than oil,
but they are drawn swords.

[22] Cast your burden on the LORD,
and he will sustain you;
he will never allow the righteous to be shaken.

[23] God, you will bring them down
to the Pit of destruction;
men of bloodshed and treachery
will not live out half their days.
But I will trust in you.

Psalm 56

A Call for God's Protection

FOR THE CHOIR DIRECTOR: ACCORDING TO "A SILENT DOVE FAR AWAY."
A *MIKTAM* OF DAVID. WHEN THE PHILISTINES SEIZED HIM IN GATH.

[1] Be gracious to me, God, for a man is trampling me;
he fights and oppresses me all day long.
[2] My adversaries trample me all day,
for many arrogantly fight against me.

[3] When I am afraid,
I will trust in you.
[4] In God, whose word I praise,
in God I trust; I will not be afraid.
What can mere mortals do to me?

[5] They twist my words all day long;
all their thoughts against me are evil.
[6] They stir up strife, they lurk,
they watch my steps
while they wait to take my life.
[7] Will they escape in spite of such sin?
God, bring down the nations in wrath.

[8] You yourself have recorded my wanderings.
Put my tears in your bottle.
Are they not in your book?
[9] Then my enemies will retreat on the day when I call.
This I know: God is for me.

10 In God, whose word I praise,
in the LORD, whose word I praise,
11 in God I trust; I will not be afraid.
What can mere humans do to me?

12 I am obligated by vows to you, God;
I will make my thanksgiving sacrifices to you.
13 For you rescued me from death,
even my feet from stumbling,
to walk before God in the light of life.

Psalm 57

Praise for God's Protection

FOR THE CHOIR DIRECTOR: "DO NOT DESTROY." A *MIKTAM* OF DAVID. WHEN HE FLED BEFORE SAUL INTO THE CAVE.

1 Be gracious to me, God, be gracious to me,
for I take refuge in you.
I will seek refuge in the shadow of your wings
until danger passes.
2 I call to God Most High,
to God who fulfills his purpose for me.
3 He reaches down from heaven and saves me,
challenging the one who tramples me. *Selah*
God sends his faithful love and truth.
4 I am surrounded by lions;
I lie down among devouring lions—
people whose teeth are spears and arrows,
whose tongues are sharp swords.
5 God, be exalted above the heavens;
let your glory be over the whole earth.
6 They prepared a net for my steps;
I was despondent.
They dug a pit ahead of me,
but they fell into it! *Selah*

7 My heart is confident, God, my heart is confident.
I will sing; I will sing praises.
8 Wake up, my soul!
Wake up, harp and lyre!
I will wake up the dawn.
9 I will praise you, Lord, among the peoples;
I will sing praises to you among the nations.
10 For your faithful love is as high as the heavens;
your faithfulness reaches the clouds.
11 God, be exalted above the heavens;
let your glory be over the whole earth.

Psalm 58

A Cry Against Injustice

FOR THE CHOIR DIRECTOR: "DO NOT DESTROY." A *MIKTAM* OF DAVID.

1 Do you really speak righteously, you mighty ones?
Do you judge people fairly?
2 No, you practice injustice in your hearts;
with your hands you weigh out violence in the land.

3 The wicked go astray from the womb;
liars wander about from birth.
4 They have venom like the venom of a snake,
like the deaf cobra that stops up its ears,
5 that does not listen to the sound of the charmers
who skillfully weave spells.

6 God, knock the teeth out of their mouths;
LORD, tear out the young lions' fangs.
7 May they vanish like water that flows by;
may they aim their blunted arrows.
8 Like a slug that moves along in slime,
like a woman's miscarried child,
may they not see the sun.

9 Before your pots can feel the heat of the thorns—
whether green or burning—
he will sweep them away.
10 The righteous one will rejoice
when he sees the retribution;
he will wash his feet in the blood of the wicked.
11 Then people will say,
"Yes, there is a reward for the righteous!
There is a God who judges on earth!"

Daily Response

Date:

WHAT ATTRIBUTES *of* GOD STOOD OUT TO ME?

HOW DO I CONNECT *with* THE HUMAN EXPERIENCES EXPRESSED *in* TODAY'S PSALMS?

Contextual markers

Poetic devices or patterns

Words or phrases for further study

HOW DO TODAY'S PSALMS GUIDE ME *in the* PRACTICES *of* LENT?

WHAT'S A VERSE *that* I WILL MEDITATE *on* TODAY?

PSALMS 59–64

DAY 18

WEEK 3

AT REST *in* GOD ALONE

Psalm 59

God Our Stronghold

FOR THE CHOIR DIRECTOR: "DO NOT DESTROY."
A *MIKTAM* OF DAVID. WHEN SAUL SENT AGENTS
TO WATCH THE HOUSE AND KILL HIM.

1 Rescue me from my enemies, my God;
protect me from those who rise up against me.
2 Rescue me from evildoers,
and save me from men of bloodshed.
3 Because look, LORD, they set an ambush for me.
Powerful men attack me,
but not because of any sin or rebellion of mine.
4 For no fault of mine,
they run and take up a position.
Awake to help me, and take notice.
5 LORD God of Armies, you are the God of Israel.
Rise up to punish all the nations;
do not show favor to any wicked traitors. *Selah*

6 They return at evening, snarling like dogs
and prowling around the city.
7 Look, they spew from their mouths—
sharp words from their lips.
"For who," they say, "will hear?"
8 But you laugh at them, LORD;
you ridicule all the nations.
9 I will keep watch for you, my strength,
because God is my stronghold.
10 My faithful God will come to meet me;
God will let me look down on my adversaries.
11 Do not kill them; otherwise, my people will forget.
By your power, make them homeless wanderers
and bring them down,
Lord, our shield.
12 For the sin of their mouths and the words of their lips,
let them be caught in their pride.
They utter curses and lies.
13 Consume them in fury;
consume them until they are gone.
Then people will know throughout the earth
that God rules over Jacob. *Selah*

14 And they return at evening, snarling like dogs
and prowling around the city.
15 They scavenge for food;
they growl if they are not satisfied.

16 But I will sing of your strength
and will joyfully proclaim
your faithful love in the morning.
For you have been a stronghold for me,
a refuge in my day of trouble.
17 To you, my strength, I sing praises,
because God is my stronghold—
my faithful God.

Psalm 60

Prayer in Difficult Times

FOR THE CHOIR DIRECTOR: ACCORDING TO "THE LILY OF TESTIMONY." A *MIKTAM* OF DAVID FOR TEACHING. WHEN HE FOUGHT WITH ARAM-NAHARAIM AND ARAM-ZOBAH, AND JOAB RETURNED AND STRUCK EDOM IN SALT VALLEY, KILLING TWELVE THOUSAND.

1 God, you have rejected us;
you have broken us down;
you have been angry. Restore us!
2 You have shaken the land and split it open.
Heal its fissures, for it shudders.
3 You have made your people suffer hardship;
you have given us wine to drink
that made us stagger.
4 You have given a signal flag to those who fear you,
so that they can flee before the archers. *Selah*
5 Save with your right hand, and answer me,
so that those you love may be rescued.

6 God has spoken in his sanctuary:
"I will celebrate!
I will divide up Shechem.
I will apportion the Valley of Succoth.
7 Gilead is mine, Manasseh is mine,
and Ephraim is my helmet;
Judah is my scepter.
8 Moab is my washbasin.
I throw my sandal on Edom;
I shout in triumph over Philistia."

9 Who will bring me to the fortified city?
Who will lead me to Edom?
10 God, haven't you rejected us?
God, you do not march out with our armies.
11 Give us aid against the foe,
for human help is worthless.
12 With God we will perform valiantly;
he will trample our foes.

Psalm 61

Security in God

FOR THE CHOIR DIRECTOR: ON STRINGED INSTRUMENTS. OF DAVID.

1 God, hear my cry;
pay attention to my prayer.
2 I call to you from the ends of the earth
when my heart is without strength.
Lead me to a rock that is high above me,
3 for you have been a refuge for me,
a strong tower in the face of the enemy.
4 I will dwell in your tent forever
and take refuge under the shelter of your wings. *Selah*

5 God, you have heard my vows;
you have given a heritage
to those who fear your name.
6 Add days to the king's life;
may his years span many generations.
7 May he sit enthroned before God forever.
Appoint faithful love and truth to guard him.
8 Then I will continually sing of your name,
fulfilling my vows day by day.

Psalm 62

Trust in God Alone

FOR THE CHOIR DIRECTOR: ACCORDING TO JEDUTHUN. A PSALM OF DAVID.

1 I am at rest in God alone;
my salvation comes from him.
2 He alone is my rock and my salvation,
my stronghold; I will never be shaken.

3 How long will you threaten a man?
Will all of you attack
as if he were a leaning wall
or a tottering fence?

NOTES

4 They only plan to bring him down
from his high position.
They take pleasure in lying;
they bless with their mouths,
but they curse inwardly. *Selah*

5 REST IN GOD ALONE, MY SOUL,
FOR MY HOPE COMES FROM HIM.

6 He alone is my rock and my salvation,
my stronghold; I will not be shaken.
7 My salvation and glory depend on God, my strong rock.
My refuge is in God.
8 Trust in him at all times, you people;
pour out your hearts before him.
God is our refuge. *Selah*

9 Common people are only a vapor;
important people, an illusion.
Together on a scale,
they weigh less than a vapor.
10 Place no trust in oppression
or false hope in robbery.
If wealth increases,
don't set your heart on it.

11 God has spoken once;
I have heard this twice:
strength belongs to God,
12 and faithful love belongs to you, Lord.
For you repay each according to his works.

Psalm 63

Praise God Who Satisfies

A PSALM OF DAVID. WHEN HE WAS IN THE WILDERNESS OF JUDAH.

1 God, you are my God; I eagerly seek you.
I thirst for you;

my body faints for you
in a land that is dry, desolate, and without water.
2 So I gaze on you in the sanctuary
to see your strength and your glory.

3 My lips will glorify you
because your faithful love is better than life.
4 So I will bless you as long as I live;
at your name, I will lift up my hands.
5 You satisfy me as with rich food;
my mouth will praise you with joyful lips.

6 When I think of you as I lie on my bed,
I meditate on you during the night watches
7 because you are my helper;
I will rejoice in the shadow of your wings.
8 I follow close to you;
your right hand holds on to me.

9 But those who intend to destroy my life
will go into the depths of the earth.
10 They will be given over to the power of the sword;
they will become a meal for jackals.
11 But the king will rejoice in God;
all who swear by him will boast,
for the mouths of liars will be shut.

Psalm 64

Protection from Evildoers

FOR THE CHOIR DIRECTOR. A PSALM OF DAVID.

1 God, hear my voice when I am in anguish.
Protect my life from the terror of the enemy.
2 Hide me from the scheming of wicked people,
from the mob of evildoers,
3 who sharpen their tongues like swords
and aim bitter words like arrows,
4 shooting from concealed places at the blameless.
They shoot at him suddenly and are not afraid.
5 They adopt an evil plan;
they talk about hiding traps and say,
"Who will see them?"
6 They devise crimes and say,
"We have perfected a secret plan."
The inner man and the heart are mysterious.

7 But God will shoot them with arrows;
suddenly, they will be wounded.
8 They will be made to stumble;
their own tongues work against them.
All who see them will shake their heads.
9 Then everyone will fear
and will tell about God's work,
for they will understand what he has done.

10 The righteous one rejoices in the LORD
and takes refuge in him;
all those who are upright in heart
will offer praise.

Daily Response

Date:

WHAT ATTRIBUTES *of* GOD STOOD OUT TO ME?

HOW DO I CONNECT *with* THE HUMAN EXPERIENCES EXPRESSED *in* TODAY'S PSALMS?

Contextual markers

Poetic devices or patterns

Words or phrases for further study

HOW DO TODAY'S PSALMS GUIDE ME *in the* PRACTICES *of* LENT?

WHAT'S A VERSE *that* I WILL MEDITATE *on* TODAY?

DAY 19

Psalms 65–68

HE HAS NOT TURNED AWAY

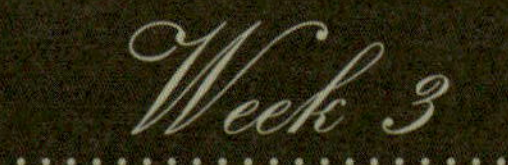

Psalm 65

God's Care for the Earth

FOR THE CHOIR DIRECTOR. A PSALM OF DAVID. A SONG.

1 Praise is rightfully yours,
God, in Zion;
vows to you will be fulfilled.
2 All humanity will come to you,
the one who hears prayer.
3 Iniquities overwhelm me;
only you can atone for our rebellions.
4 How happy is the one you choose
and bring near to live in your courts!
We will be satisfied with the goodness of your house,
the holiness of your temple.

5 You answer us in righteousness,
with awe-inspiring works,
God of our salvation,
the hope of all the ends of the earth
and of the distant seas.
6 You establish the mountains by your power;
you are robed with strength.
7 You silence the roar of the seas,
the roar of their waves,
and the tumult of the nations.
8 Those who live far away are awed by your signs;
you make east and west shout for joy.

9 You visit the earth and water it abundantly,
enriching it greatly.
God's stream is filled with water,
for you prepare the earth in this way,
providing people with grain.
10 You soften it with showers and bless its growth,
soaking its furrows and leveling its ridges.
11 You crown the year with your goodness;
your carts overflow with plenty.
12 The wilderness pastures overflow,
and the hills are robed with joy.
13 The pastures are clothed with flocks
and the valleys covered with grain.
They shout in triumph; indeed, they sing.

NOTES

Psalm 66

Praise for God's Mighty Acts

FOR THE CHOIR DIRECTOR. A SONG. A PSALM.

1 Let the whole earth shout joyfully to God!
2 Sing about the glory of his name;
make his praise glorious.
3 Say to God, "How awe-inspiring are your works!
Your enemies will cringe before you
because of your great strength.
4 The whole earth will worship you
and sing praise to you.
They will sing praise to your name." *Selah*

5 Come and see the wonders of God;
his acts for humanity are awe-inspiring.
6 He turned the sea into dry land,
and they crossed the river on foot.
There we rejoiced in him.
7 He rules forever by his might;
he keeps his eye on the nations.
The rebellious should not exalt themselves. *Selah*
8 Bless our God, you peoples;
let the sound of his praise be heard.
9 He keeps us alive
and does not allow our feet to slip.

10 For you, God, tested us;
you refined us as silver is refined.
11 You lured us into a trap;
you placed burdens on our backs.
12 You let men ride over our heads;
we went through fire and water,
but you brought us out to abundance.

13 I will enter your house with burnt offerings;
I will pay you my vows
14 that my lips promised
and my mouth spoke during my distress.
15 I will offer you fattened sheep as burnt offerings,
with the fragrant smoke of rams;
I will sacrifice bulls with goats. *Selah*

16 Come and listen, all who fear God,
and I will tell what he has done for me.
17 I cried out to him with my mouth,
and praise was on my tongue.
18 If I had been aware of malice in my heart,
the Lord would not have listened.
19 However, God has listened;
he has paid attention to the sound of my prayer.
20 Blessed be God!
He has not turned away my prayer
or turned his faithful love from me.

Psalm 67

All Will Praise God

FOR THE CHOIR DIRECTOR: WITH STRINGED INSTRUMENTS. A PSALM. A SONG.

1 May God be gracious to us and bless us;
may he make his face shine upon us *Selah*
2 so that your way may be known on earth,
your salvation among all nations.

3 Let the peoples praise you, God;
let all the peoples praise you.
4 Let the nations rejoice and shout for joy,
for you judge the peoples with fairness
and lead the nations on earth. *Selah*
5 Let the peoples praise you, God,
let all the peoples praise you.

6 The earth has produced its harvest;
God, our God, blesses us.
7 God will bless us,
and all the ends of the earth will fear him.

Psalm 68

God's Majestic Power

FOR THE CHOIR DIRECTOR. A PSALM OF DAVID. A SONG.

1 God arises. His enemies scatter,
and those who hate him flee from his presence.
2 As smoke is blown away,
so you blow them away.

As wax melts before the fire,
so the wicked are destroyed before God.
3 But the righteous are glad;
they rejoice before God and celebrate with joy.

4 Sing to God! Sing praises to his name.
Exalt him who rides on the clouds—

HIS NAME IS THE LORD—AND CELEBRATE BEFORE HIM.

5 God in his holy dwelling is
a father of the fatherless
and a champion of widows.
6 God provides homes for those who are deserted.
He leads out the prisoners to prosperity,
but the rebellious live in a scorched land.

7 God, when you went out before your people,
when you marched through the desert, *Selah*
8 the earth trembled and the skies poured rain
before God, the God of Sinai,
before God, the God of Israel.
9 You, God, showered abundant rain;
you revived your inheritance when it languished.
10 Your people settled in it;
God, you provided for the poor by your goodness.

11 The Lord gave the command;
a great company of women brought the good news:
12 "The kings of the armies flee—they flee!"
She who stays at home divides the spoil.
13 While you lie among the sheep pens,
the wings of a dove are covered with silver,
and its feathers with glistening gold.
14 When the Almighty scattered kings in the land,
it snowed on Zalmon.

15 Mount Bashan is God's towering mountain;
Mount Bashan is a mountain of many peaks.
16 Why gaze with envy, you mountain peaks,
at the mountain God desired for his abode?
The Lord will dwell there forever!
17 God's chariots are tens of thousands,
thousands and thousands;

the Lord is among them in the sanctuary
as he was at Sinai.
18 You ascended to the heights, taking away captives;
you received gifts from people,
even from the rebellious,
so that the LORD God might dwell there.

19 Blessed be the Lord!
Day after day he bears our burdens;
God is our salvation. *Selah*
20 Our God is a God of salvation,
and escape from death belongs to the LORD my Lord.
21 Surely God crushes the heads of his enemies,
the hairy brow of one who goes on in his guilty acts.
22 The Lord said, "I will bring them back from Bashan;
I will bring them back from the depths of the sea
23 so that your foot may wade in blood
and your dogs' tongues may have their share
from the enemies."
24 People have seen your procession, God,
the procession of my God,
my King, in the sanctuary.
25 Singers lead the way,
with musicians following;
among them are young women
playing tambourines.
26 Bless God in the assemblies;
bless the LORD from the fountain of Israel.
27 There is Benjamin, the youngest, leading them,
the rulers of Judah in their assembly,
the rulers of Zebulun, the rulers of Naphtali.

28 Your God has decreed your strength.
Show your strength, God,
you who have acted on our behalf.
29 Because of your temple at Jerusalem,
kings will bring tribute to you.
30 Rebuke the beast in the reeds,
the herd of bulls with the calves of the peoples.
Trample underfoot those with bars of silver.
Scatter the peoples who take pleasure in war.
31 Ambassadors will come from Egypt;
Cush will stretch out its hands to God.

32 Sing to God, you kingdoms of the earth;
sing praise to the Lord, *Selah*
33 to him who rides in the ancient, highest heavens.
Look, he thunders with his powerful voice!
34 Ascribe power to God.
His majesty is over Israel;
his power is among the clouds.
35 God, you are awe-inspiring in your sanctuaries.
The God of Israel gives power and strength to his people.
Blessed be God!

Daily Response

Date:

WHAT ATTRIBUTES *of* GOD STOOD OUT TO ME?

HOW DO I CONNECT *with* THE HUMAN EXPERIENCES EXPRESSED *in* TODAY'S PSALMS?

Contextual markers

Poetic devices or patterns

Words or phrases for further study

HOW DO TODAY'S PSALMS GUIDE ME *in the* PRACTICES *of* LENT?

WHAT'S A VERSE *that* I WILL MEDITATE *on* TODAY?

Week Three *Response*

Use Psalm 46 to respond in prayer, allowing the words of Scripture to guide your prayer. Talk to the Lord about whatever the psalm brings to mind. Refer back to the example on page 46 if you need to.

Psalm 46

God Our Refuge

FOR THE CHOIR DIRECTOR. A SONG OF THE SONS OF KORAH. ACCORDING TO *ALAMOTH*.

1 God is our refuge and strength,
a helper who is always found
in times of trouble.

2 Therefore we will not be afraid,
though the earth trembles
and the mountains topple
into the depths of the seas,

3 though its water roars and foams
and the mountains quake with its turmoil. *Selah*

4 There is a river—
its streams delight the city of God,
the holy dwelling place of the Most High.

5 God is within her; she will not be toppled.
God will help her when the morning dawns.

6 Nations rage, kingdoms topple;
the earth melts when he lifts his voice.

7 The LORD of Armies is with us;
the God of Jacob is our stronghold. *Selah*

8 Come, see the works of the LORD,
who brings devastation on the earth.

9 He makes wars cease throughout the earth.
He shatters bows and cuts spears to pieces;
he sets wagons ablaze.

10 "Stop fighting, and know that I am God,
exalted among the nations, exalted on the earth."

11 The LORD of Armies is with us;
the God of Jacob is our stronghold. *Selah*

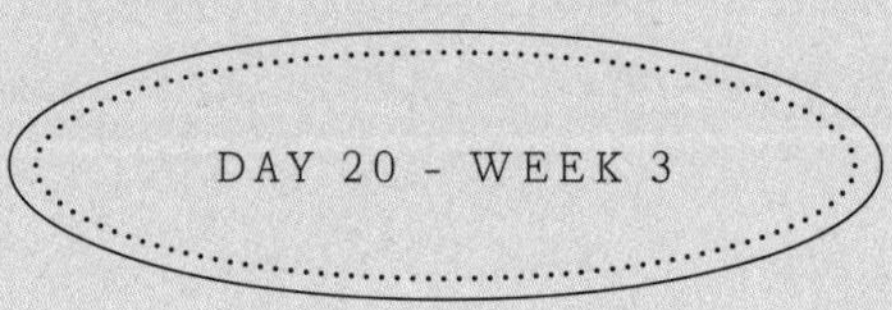

GRACE *Day*

TAKE EACH SATURDAY *to* CATCH UP ON YOUR READING, PRAY, *and* REST *in the* PRESENCE *of the* LORD *with* PASSAGES *from* SCRIPTURE THAT WE TRADITIONALLY READ DURING *the* LENTEN SEASON.

"This is my servant; I strengthen him,
this is my chosen one; I delight in him.
I have put my Spirit on him;
he will bring justice to the nations.
He will not cry out or shout
or make his voice heard in the streets.
He will not break a bruised reed,
and he will not put out a smoldering wick;
he will faithfully bring justice.
He will not grow weak or be discouraged
until he has established justice on earth.
The coasts and islands will wait for his instruction."

ISAIAH 42:1–4

DAY 21 - WEEK 3

WEEKLY TRUTH

SCRIPTURE IS GOD BREATHED *and* TRUE. WHEN WE MEMORIZE IT, WE CARRY HIS WORD *with* US WHEREVER WE GO.

EACH SUNDAY DURING THIS PLAN, WE ARE READING *a* DIFFERENT HALLEL PSALM *and* MEMORIZING ONE *of* ITS VERSES.

THIS WEEK, MEMORIZE PSALM 115:1 AS YOU MEDITATE *on the* PSALM *as a* WHOLE.

Psalm 115

Glory to God Alone

[1] Not to us, LORD, not to us,
but to your name give glory
because of your faithful love, because of your truth.
[2] Why should the nations say,
"Where is their God?"
[3] Our God is in heaven
and does whatever he pleases.

[4] Their idols are silver and gold,
made by human hands.
[5] They have mouths but cannot speak,
eyes, but cannot see.
[6] They have ears but cannot hear,
noses, but cannot smell.
[7] They have hands but cannot feel,
feet, but cannot walk.
They cannot make a sound with their throats.
[8] Those who make them are just like them,
as are all who trust in them.

[9] Israel, trust in the LORD!
He is their help and shield.
[10] House of Aaron, trust in the LORD!
He is their help and shield.
[11] You who fear the LORD, trust in the LORD!
He is their help and shield.
[12] The LORD remembers us and will bless us.
He will bless the house of Israel;
he will bless the house of Aaron;
[13] he will bless those who fear the LORD—
small and great alike.

[14] May the LORD add to your numbers,
both yours and your children's.
[15] May you be blessed by the LORD,
the Maker of heaven and earth.
[16] The heavens are the LORD's,
but the earth he has given to the human race.
[17] It is not the dead who praise the LORD,
nor any of those descending into the silence
of death.
[18] But we will bless the LORD,
both now and forever.
Hallelujah!

SEE TIPS FOR MEMORIZING SCRIPTURE ON PAGE 272.

PSALMS 69–72

ANSWER ME *with* YOUR SURE SALVATION

But as for me, LORD, my prayer to you is for a time of favor. In your abundant, faithful love, God, answer me with your sure salvation.

Psalm 69:13

Psalm 69

A Plea for Rescue

FOR THE CHOIR DIRECTOR: ACCORDING TO "THE LILIES."
OF DAVID.

1 Save me, God,
for the water has risen to my neck.
2 I have sunk in deep mud, and there is no footing;
I have come into deep water,
and a flood sweeps over me.
3 I am weary from my crying;
my throat is parched.
My eyes fail, looking for my God.
4 Those who hate me without cause
are more numerous than the hairs of my head;
my deceitful enemies, who would destroy me,
are powerful.
Though I did not steal, I must repay.

5 God, you know my foolishness,
and my guilty acts are not hidden from you.
6 Do not let those who put their hope in you
be disgraced because of me,
Lord God of Armies;
do not let those who seek you
be humiliated because of me,
God of Israel.
7 For I have endured insults because of you,
and shame has covered my face.
8 I have become a stranger to my brothers
and a foreigner to my mother's sons
9 because zeal for your house has consumed me,
and the insults of those who insult you
have fallen on me.
10 I mourned and fasted,
but it brought me insults.
11 I wore sackcloth as my clothing,
and I was a joke to them.
12 Those who sit at the city gate talk about me,
and drunkards make up songs about me.

13 But as for me, Lord,
my prayer to you is for a time of favor.
In your abundant, faithful love, God,
answer me with your sure salvation.
14 Rescue me from the miry mud; don't let me sink.
Let me be rescued from those who hate me
and from the deep water.
15 Don't let the floodwaters sweep over me
or the deep swallow me up;
don't let the Pit close its mouth over me.
16 Answer me, Lord,
for your faithful love is good.
In keeping with your abundant compassion,
turn to me.
17 Don't hide your face from your servant,
for I am in distress.
Answer me quickly!
18 Come near to me and redeem me;
ransom me because of my enemies.

19 You know the insults I endure—
my shame and disgrace.
You are aware of all my adversaries.
20 Insults have broken my heart,
and I am in despair.
I waited for sympathy,
but there was none;
for comforters, but found no one.
21 Instead, they gave me gall for my food,
and for my thirst
they gave me vinegar to drink.

22 Let their table set before them be a snare,
and let it be a trap for their allies.
23 Let their eyes grow too dim to see,
and let their hips continually quake.
24 Pour out your rage on them,
and let your burning anger overtake them.
25 Make their fortification desolate;
may no one live in their tents.
26 For they persecute the one you struck
and talk about the pain of those you wounded.
27 Charge them with crime on top of crime;
do not let them share in your righteousness.

28 Let them be erased from the book of life
and not be recorded with the righteous.

29 But as for me—poor and in pain—
let your salvation protect me, God.
30 I will praise God's name with song
and exalt him with thanksgiving.
31 That will please the LORD more than an ox,
more than a bull with horns and hooves.
32 The humble will see it and rejoice.
You who seek God, take heart!
33 For the LORD listens to the needy
and does not despise
his own who are prisoners.

34 Let heaven and earth praise him,
the seas and everything that moves in them,
35 for God will save Zion
and build up the cities of Judah.
They will live there and possess it.
36 The descendants of his servants will inherit it,
and those who love his name will live in it.

Psalm 70

A Call for Deliverance

FOR THE CHOIR DIRECTOR. OF DAVID.
TO BRING REMEMBRANCE.

1 God, hurry to rescue me.
LORD, hurry to help me!

2 Let those who seek to kill me
be disgraced and confounded;
let those who wish me harm
be turned back and humiliated.
3 Let those who say, "Aha, aha!"
retreat because of their shame.

4 Let all who seek you rejoice and be glad in you;
let those who love your salvation
continually say, "God is great!"
5 I am oppressed and needy;
hurry to me, God.
You are my help and my deliverer;
LORD, do not delay.

Psalm 71

God's Help in Old Age

1 LORD, I seek refuge in you;
let me never be disgraced.
2 In your justice, rescue and deliver me;
listen closely to me and save me.
3 Be a rock of refuge for me,
where I can always go.
Give the command to save me,
for you are my rock and fortress.
4 Deliver me, my God, from the power of the wicked,
from the grasp of the unjust and oppressive.
5 For you are my hope, Lord GOD,
my confidence from my youth.
6 I have leaned on you from birth;
you took me from my mother's womb.
My praise is always about you.
7 I am like a miraculous sign to many,
and you are my strong refuge.
8 My mouth is full of praise
and honor to you all day long.

9 Don't discard me in my old age.
As my strength fails, do not abandon me.
10 For my enemies talk about me,
and those who spy on me plot together,
11 saying, "God has abandoned him;
chase him and catch him,
for there is no one to rescue him."
12 God, do not be far from me;
my God, hurry to help me.
13 May my adversaries be disgraced and destroyed;
may those who intend to harm me
be covered with disgrace and humiliation.
14 But I will hope continually
and will praise you more and more.
15 My mouth will tell about your righteousness
and your salvation all day long,
though I cannot sum them up.
16 I come because of the mighty acts of the Lord GOD;
I will proclaim your righteousness, yours alone.

17 God, you have taught me from my youth,
and I still proclaim your wondrous works.

[18] Even while I am old and gray,
God, do not abandon me,
while I proclaim your power
to another generation,
your strength to all who are to come.
[19] Your righteousness reaches the heights, God,
you who have done great things;
God, who is like you?
[20] You caused me to experience
many troubles and misfortunes,
but you will revive me again.
You will bring me up again,
even from the depths of the earth.
[21] You will increase my honor
and comfort me once again.
[22] Therefore, I will praise you with a harp
for your faithfulness, my God;
I will sing to you with a lyre,
Holy One of Israel.
[23] My lips will shout for joy
when I sing praise to you
because you have redeemed me.
[24] Therefore, my tongue will proclaim
your righteousness all day long,
for those who intend to harm me
will be disgraced and confounded.

Psalm 72

A Prayer for the King

OF SOLOMON.

[1] God, give your justice to the king
and your righteousness to the king's son.
[2] He will judge your people with righteousness
and your afflicted ones with justice.
[3] May the mountains bring well-being to the people
and the hills, righteousness.
[4] May he vindicate the afflicted among the people,
help the poor,
and crush the oppressor.

[5] May they fear you while the sun endures
and as long as the moon, throughout all generations.
[6] May the king be like rain that falls on the cut grass,

like spring showers that water the earth.
7 May the righteous flourish in his days
and well-being abound
until the moon is no more.

8 May he rule from sea to sea
and from the Euphrates
to the ends of the earth.
9 May desert tribes kneel before him
and his enemies lick the dust.
10 May the kings of Tarshish
and the coasts and islands bring tribute,
the kings of Sheba and Seba offer gifts.
11 Let all kings bow in homage to him,
all nations serve him.

12 For he will rescue the poor who cry out
and the afflicted who have no helper.
13 He will have pity on the poor and helpless
and save the lives of the poor.
14 He will redeem them from oppression and violence,
for their lives are precious in his sight.

15 May he live long!
May gold from Sheba be given to him.
May prayer be offered for him continually,
and may he be blessed all day long.
16 May there be plenty of grain in the land;
may it wave on the tops of the mountains.
May its crops be like Lebanon.
May people flourish in the cities
like the grass of the field.
17 May his name endure forever;
as long as the sun shines,
may his fame increase.
May all nations be blessed by him
and call him blessed.

18 Blessed be the LORD God, the God of Israel,
who alone does wonders.
19 Blessed be his glorious name forever;
the whole earth is filled with his glory.
Amen and amen.
20 The prayers of David son of Jesse are concluded.

Daily Response

Date:

WHAT ATTRIBUTES *of* GOD STOOD OUT TO ME?

HOW DO I CONNECT *with* THE HUMAN EXPERIENCES EXPRESSED *in* TODAY'S PSALMS?

Contextual markers

Poetic devices or patterns

Words or phrases for further study

HOW DO TODAY'S PSALMS GUIDE ME *in the* PRACTICES *of* LENT?

WHAT'S A VERSE *that* I WILL MEDITATE *on* TODAY?

GOD IS THE STRENGTH OF MY HEART

Psalms 73–76

MY FLESH *and* MY HEART MAY FAIL, *but* GOD IS *the* STRENGTH *of* MY HEART, MY PORTION FOREVER.

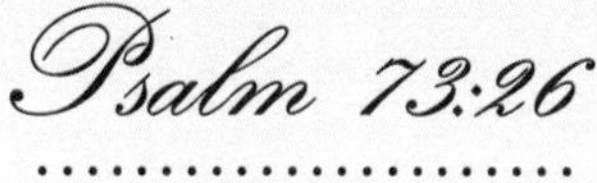

DAY 23  WEEK 4

Psalm 73

God's Ways Vindicated

A PSALM OF ASAPH.

1 God is indeed good to Israel,
to the pure in heart.
2 But as for me, my feet almost slipped;
my steps nearly went astray.
3 For I envied the arrogant;
I saw the prosperity of the wicked.

4 They have an easy time until they die,
and their bodies are well fed.
5 They are not in trouble like others;
they are not afflicted like most people.
6 Therefore, pride is their necklace,
and violence covers them like a garment.
7 Their eyes bulge out from fatness;
the imaginations of their hearts run wild.
8 They mock, and they speak maliciously;
they arrogantly threaten oppression.
9 They set their mouths against heaven,
and their tongues strut across the earth.
10 Therefore his people turn to them
and drink in their overflowing words.
11 The wicked say, "How can God know?
Does the Most High know everything?"
12 Look at them—the wicked!
They are always at ease,
and they increase their wealth.

13 Did I purify my heart
and wash my hands in innocence for nothing?
14 For I am afflicted all day long
and punished every morning.
15 If I had decided to say these things aloud,
I would have betrayed your people.
16 When I tried to understand all this,
it seemed hopeless
17 until I entered God's sanctuary.
Then I understood their destiny.
18 Indeed, you put them in slippery places;
you make them fall into ruin.
19 How suddenly they become a desolation!
They come to an end, swept away by terrors.
20 Like one waking from a dream,
Lord, when arising, you will despise their image.

21 When I became embittered
and my innermost being was wounded,
22 I was stupid and didn't understand;
I was an unthinking animal toward you.
23 Yet I am always with you;
you hold my right hand.
24 You guide me with your counsel,
and afterward you will take me up in glory.
25 Who do I have in heaven but you?
And I desire nothing on earth but you.
26 My flesh and my heart may fail,
but God is the strength of my heart,
my portion forever.
27 Those far from you will certainly perish;
you destroy all who are unfaithful to you.

28 BUT AS FOR ME, GOD'S PRESENCE
IS MY GOOD.
I HAVE MADE THE LORD GOD
MY REFUGE,
SO I CAN TELL ABOUT ALL YOU DO.

Psalm 74

Prayer for Israel

A *MASKIL* OF ASAPH.

1 Why have you rejected us forever, God?
Why does your anger burn
against the sheep of your pasture?
2 Remember your congregation,
which you purchased long ago
and redeemed as the tribe for your own possession.
Remember Mount Zion where you dwell.
3 Make your way to the perpetual ruins,
to all that the enemy has destroyed in the sanctuary.
4 Your adversaries roared in the meeting place
where you met with us.

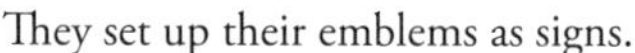

They set up their emblems as signs.
5 It was like men in a thicket of trees,
wielding axes,
6 then smashing all the carvings
with hatchets and picks.
7 They set your sanctuary on fire;
they utterly desecrated
the dwelling place of your name.
8 They said in their hearts,
"Let's oppress them relentlessly."
They burned every place throughout the land
where God met with us.
9 There are no signs for us to see.
There is no longer a prophet.
And none of us knows how long this will last.
10 God, how long will the enemy mock?
Will the foe insult your name forever?
11 Why do you hold back your hand?
Stretch out your right hand and destroy them!

12 God my King is from ancient times,
performing saving acts on the earth.
13 You divided the sea with your strength;
you smashed the heads of the sea monsters in the water;
14 you crushed the heads of Leviathan;
you fed him to the creatures of the desert.
15 You opened up springs and streams;
you dried up ever-flowing rivers.
16 The day is yours, also the night;
you established the moon and the sun.
17 You set all the boundaries of the earth;
you made summer and winter.

18 Remember this: the enemy has mocked the LORD,
and a foolish people has insulted your name.
19 Do not give to beasts the life of your dove;
do not forget the lives of your poor people forever.
20 Consider the covenant,
for the dark places of the land are full of violence.
21 Do not let the oppressed turn away in shame;
let the poor and needy praise your name.
22 Rise up, God, champion your cause!
Remember the insults

that fools bring against you all day long.
23 Do not forget the clamor of your adversaries,
the tumult of your opponents that goes up constantly.

Psalm 75

God Judges the Wicked

FOR THE CHOIR DIRECTOR: "DO NOT DESTROY."
A PSALM OF ASAPH. A SONG.

1 We give thanks to you, God;
we give thanks to you, for your name is near.
People tell about your wondrous works.

2 "When I choose a time,
I will judge fairly.
3 When the earth and all its inhabitants shake,
I am the one who steadies its pillars. *Selah*
4 I say to the boastful, 'Do not boast,'
and to the wicked, 'Do not lift up your horn.
5 Do not lift up your horn against heaven
or speak arrogantly.'"

6 Exaltation does not come
from the east, the west, or the desert,
7 for God is the Judge:
He brings down one and exalts another.
8 For there is a cup in the LORD's hand,
full of wine blended with spices, and he pours from it.
All the wicked of the earth will drink,
draining it to the dregs.

9 As for me, I will tell about him forever;
I will sing praise to the God of Jacob.

10 "I will cut off all the horns of the wicked,
but the horns of the righteous will be lifted up."

Psalm 76

God, the Powerful Judge

FOR THE CHOIR DIRECTOR: WITH STRINGED INSTRUMENTS.
A PSALM OF ASAPH. A SONG.

1 God is known in Judah;
his name is great in Israel.
2 His tent is in Salem,
his dwelling place in Zion.
3 There he shatters the bow's flaming arrows,
the shield, the sword, and the weapons of war. *Selah*

4 You are resplendent and majestic
coming down from the mountains of prey.
5 The brave-hearted have been plundered;
they have slipped into their final sleep.
None of the warriors was able to lift a hand.
6 At your rebuke, God of Jacob,
both chariot and horse lay still.

7 And you—you are to be feared.
When you are angry,
who can stand before you?
8 From heaven you pronounced judgment.
The earth feared and grew quiet
9 when God rose up to judge
and to save all the lowly of the earth. *Selah*
10 Even human wrath will praise you;
you will clothe yourself
with the wrath that remains.

11 Make and keep your vows
to the LORD your God;
let all who are around him bring tribute
to the awe-inspiring one.
12 He humbles the spirit of leaders;
he is feared by the kings of the earth.

Daily Response

Date:

WHAT ATTRIBUTES *of* GOD STOOD OUT TO ME?

HOW DO I CONNECT *with* THE HUMAN EXPERIENCES EXPRESSED *in* TODAY'S PSALMS?

Contextual markers

Poetic devices or patterns

Words or phrases for further study

HOW DO TODAY'S PSALMS GUIDE ME *in the* PRACTICES *of* LENT?

WHAT'S A VERSE *that* I WILL MEDITATE *on* TODAY?

I WILL REMEMBER *the* LORD'S WORKS

Psalms 77–79

DAY 24  WEEK 4

Psalm 77

Confidence in a Time of Crisis

FOR THE CHOIR DIRECTOR: ACCORDING TO JEDUTHUN. OF ASAPH. A PSALM.

1 I cry aloud to God,
aloud to God, and he will hear me.
2 I sought the Lord in my day of trouble.
My hands were continually lifted up
all night long;
I refused to be comforted.
3 I think of God; I groan;
I meditate; my spirit becomes weak. *Selah*

4 You have kept me from closing my eyes;
I am troubled and cannot speak.
5 I consider days of old,
years long past.
6 At night I remember my music;
I meditate in my heart, and my spirit ponders.

7 "Will the Lord reject forever
and never again show favor?
8 Has his faithful love ceased forever?
Is his promise at an end for all generations?
9 Has God forgotten to be gracious?
Has he in anger withheld his compassion?" *Selah*

10 So I say, "I am grieved
that the right hand of the Most High has changed."
11 I will remember the LORD's works;
yes, I will remember your ancient wonders.
12 I will reflect on all you have done
and meditate on your actions.

13 God, your way is holy.
What god is great like God?
14 You are the God who works wonders;
you revealed your strength among the peoples.
15 With power you redeemed your people,
the descendants of Jacob and Joseph. *Selah*

16 The water saw you, God.
The water saw you; it trembled.
Even the depths shook.
17 The clouds poured down water.
The storm clouds thundered;
your arrows flashed back and forth.
18 The sound of your thunder was in the whirlwind;
lightning lit up the world.
The earth shook and quaked.
19 Your way went through the sea
and your path through the vast water,
but your footprints were unseen.
20 You led your people like a flock
by the hand of Moses and Aaron.

Psalm 78

Lessons from Israel's Past

A *MASKIL* OF ASAPH.

1 My people, hear my instruction;
listen to the words from my mouth.
2 I will declare wise sayings;
I will speak mysteries from the past—
3 things we have heard and known
and that our ancestors have passed down to us.
4 We will not hide them from their children,
but will tell a future generation
the praiseworthy acts of the LORD,
his might, and the wondrous works
he has performed.
5 He established a testimony in Jacob
and set up a law in Israel,
which he commanded our ancestors
to teach to their children
6 so that a future generation—
children yet to be born—might know.
They were to rise and tell their children
7 so that they might put their confidence in God
and not forget God's works,
but keep his commands.
8 Then they would not be like their ancestors,

a stubborn and rebellious generation,
a generation whose heart was not loyal
and whose spirit was not faithful to God.

9 The Ephraimite archers turned back
on the day of battle.
10 They did not keep God's covenant
and refused to live by his law.
11 They forgot what he had done,
the wondrous works he had shown them.
12 He worked wonders in the sight of their ancestors
in the land of Egypt, the territory of Zoan.
13 He split the sea and brought them across;
the water stood firm like a wall.
14 He led them with a cloud by day
and with a fiery light throughout the night.
15 He split rocks in the wilderness
and gave them drink as abundant as the depths.
16 He brought streams out of the stone
and made water flow down like rivers.

17 But they continued to sin against him,
rebelling in the desert against the Most High.
18 They deliberately tested God,
demanding the food they craved.
19 They spoke against God, saying,
"Is God able to provide food in the wilderness?
20 Look! He struck the rock and water gushed out;
torrents overflowed.
But can he also provide bread
or furnish meat for his people?"
21 Therefore, the Lord heard and became furious;
then fire broke out against Jacob,
and anger flared up against Israel
22 because they did not believe God
or rely on his salvation.
23 He gave a command to the clouds above
and opened the doors of heaven.
24 He rained manna for them to eat;
he gave them grain from heaven.
25 People ate the bread of angels.
He sent them an abundant supply of food.
26 He made the east wind blow in the skies
and drove the south wind by his might.
27 He rained meat on them like dust,
and winged birds like the sand of the seas.
28 He made them fall in the camp,
all around the tents.
29 The people ate and were completely satisfied,
for he gave them what they craved.
30 Before they had turned from what they craved,
while the food was still in their mouths,
31 God's anger flared up against them,
and he killed some of their best men.
He struck down Israel's fit young men.

32 Despite all this, they kept sinning
and did not believe his wondrous works.
33 He made their days end in futility,
their years in sudden disaster.
34 When he killed some of them,
the rest began to seek him;
they repented and searched for God.

35 THEY REMEMBERED THAT
GOD WAS THEIR ROCK,
THE MOST HIGH GOD,
THEIR REDEEMER.

36 But they deceived him with their mouths,
they lied to him with their tongues,
37 their hearts were insincere toward him,
and they were unfaithful to his covenant.
38 Yet he was compassionate;
he atoned for their iniquity
and did not destroy them.
He often turned his anger aside
and did not unleash all his wrath.
39 He remembered that they were only flesh,
a wind that passes and does not return.

40 How often they rebelled against him
in the wilderness
and grieved him in the desert.
41 They constantly tested God
and provoked the Holy One of Israel.
42 They did not remember his power shown
on the day he redeemed them from the foe,

43 when he performed his miraculous signs in Egypt
and his wonders in the territory of Zoan.
44 He turned their rivers into blood,
and they could not drink from their streams.
45 He sent among them swarms of flies,
which fed on them,
and frogs, which devastated them.
46 He gave their crops to the caterpillar
and the fruit of their labor to the locust.
47 He killed their vines with hail
and their sycamore fig trees with a flood.
48 He handed over their livestock to hail
and their cattle to lightning bolts.
49 He sent his burning anger against them:
fury, indignation, and calamity—
a band of deadly messengers.
50 He cleared a path for his anger.
He did not spare them from death
but delivered their lives to the plague.
51 He struck all the firstborn in Egypt,
the first progeny of the tents of Ham.
52 He led his people out like sheep
and guided them like a flock in the wilderness.
53 He led them safely, and they were not afraid;
but the sea covered their enemies.
54 He brought them to his holy territory,
to the mountain his right hand acquired.
55 He drove out nations before them.
He apportioned their inheritance by lot
and settled the tribes of Israel in their tents.

56 But they rebelliously tested the Most High God,
for they did not keep his decrees.
57 They treacherously turned away like their ancestors;
they became warped like a faulty bow.
58 They enraged him with their high places
and provoked his jealousy with their carved images.
59 God heard and became furious;
he completely rejected Israel.
60 He abandoned the tabernacle at Shiloh,
the tent where he resided among mankind.
61 He gave up his strength to captivity
and his splendor to the hand of a foe.

NOTES

[62] He surrendered his people to the sword
because he was enraged with his heritage.
[63] Fire consumed his chosen young men,
and his young women had no wedding songs.
[64] His priests fell by the sword,
and the widows could not lament.

[65] The Lord awoke as if from sleep,
like a warrior from the effects of wine.
[66] He beat back his foes;
he gave them lasting disgrace.
[67] He rejected the tent of Joseph
and did not choose the tribe of Ephraim.
[68] He chose instead the tribe of Judah,
Mount Zion, which he loved.
[69] He built his sanctuary like the heights,
like the earth that he established forever.
[70] He chose David his servant
and took him from the sheep pens;
[71] he brought him from tending ewes
to be shepherd over his people Jacob—
over Israel, his inheritance.
[72] He shepherded them with a pure heart
and guided them with his skillful hands.

Psalm 79

Faith amid Confusion

A PSALM OF ASAPH.

[1] God, the nations have invaded your inheritance,
desecrated your holy temple,
and turned Jerusalem into ruins.
[2] They gave the corpses of your servants
to the birds of the sky for food,
the flesh of your faithful ones
to the beasts of the earth.
[3] They poured out their blood
like water all around Jerusalem,
and there was no one to bury them.
[4] We have become an object of reproach
to our neighbors,
a source of mockery and ridicule
to those around us.

[5] How long, LORD? Will you be angry forever?
Will your jealousy keep burning like fire?
[6] Pour out your wrath on the nations
that don't acknowledge you,
on the kingdoms that don't call on your name,
[7] for they have devoured Jacob
and devastated his homeland.
[8] Do not hold past iniquities against us;
let your compassion come to us quickly,
for we have become very weak.

[9] God of our salvation, help us,
for the glory of your name.
Rescue us and atone for our sins,
for your name's sake.
[10] Why should the nations ask,
"Where is their God?"
Before our eyes,
let vengeance for the shed blood of your servants
be known among the nations.
[11] Let the groans of the prisoners reach you;
according to your great power,
preserve those condemned to die.

[12] Pay back sevenfold to our neighbors
the reproach they have hurled at you, Lord.
[13] Then we, your people, the sheep of your pasture,
will thank you forever;
we will declare your praise
to generation after generation.

Daily Response

Date:

WHAT ATTRIBUTES *of* GOD STOOD OUT TO ME?

HOW DO I CONNECT *with* THE HUMAN EXPERIENCES EXPRESSED *in* TODAY'S PSALMS?

Contextual markers

Poetic devices or patterns

Words or phrases for further study

HOW DO TODAY'S PSALMS GUIDE ME *in the* PRACTICES *of* LENT?

WHAT'S A VERSE *that* I WILL MEDITATE *on* TODAY?

"I WILL" STATEMENTS *in the* PSALMS

The book of Psalms gives us many examples of people interacting with God on a deeply emotional level, inviting us to expand the intimacy and authenticity of our relationship with Him. We have selected a few of the instances where writers of the psalms offer statements of faithfulness to and dependence upon God even in the midst of great personal suffering or grief.

As you pause and meditate on the list on the following page, we invite you to integrate the statements that are impactful to you in your own time with God, anchoring your story in the comforting truth of God's Word.

"I WILL" STATEMENTS *in the* PSALMS

Ps 4:8	I will both lie down and sleep in peace, for you alone, LORD, make me live in safety.
Ps 16:7	I will bless the LORD who counsels me—even at night when my thoughts trouble me.
Ps 17:15	...when I awake, I will be satisfied with your presence.
Ps 22:22	I will proclaim your name to my brothers and sisters.
Ps 23:6	...I will dwell in the house of the LORD as long as I live.
Ps 27:8	LORD, I will seek your face.
Ps 27:13	I am certain that I will see the LORD's goodness in the land of the living.
Ps 32:5	I said, "I will confess my transgressions to the LORD," and you forgave the guilt of my sin.
Ps 34:1	I will bless the LORD at all times; his praise will always be on my lips.
Ps 43:4	Then I will come to the altar of God, to God, my greatest joy.
Ps 52:9	I will praise you forever for what you have done.
Ps 52:9	...I will put my hope in your name, for it is good.
Ps 56:3	When I am afraid, I will trust in you.
Ps 57:1	I will seek refuge in the shadow of your wings until danger passes.
Ps 62:2	He alone is my rock and my salvation, my stronghold; I will never be shaken.
Ps 63:3	My lips will glorify you because your faithful love is better than life.

Ps 66:16 …I will tell what he has done for me.

Ps 71:14 But I will hope continually and will praise you more and more.

Ps 77:11 I will remember the LORD's works…

Ps 85:8 I will listen to what God will say.

Ps 92:4 I will shout for joy because of the works of your hands.

Ps 101:2 I will live with a heart of integrity in my house.

Ps 101:3 I will not let anything worthless guide me.

Ps 108:1 I will sing praises with the whole of my being.

Ps 109:30 I will fervently thank the LORD with my mouth.

Ps 116:2 Because he has turned his ear to me, I will call out to him as long as I live.

Ps 118:6 The LORD is for me; I will not be afraid. What can a mere mortal do to me?

Ps 119:16 I will delight in your statutes; I will not forget your word.

Ps 119:34 Help me understand your instruction, and I will obey it and follow it with all my heart.

Ps 139:14 I will praise you because I have been remarkably and wondrously made.

Ps 145:2 I will bless you every day; I will praise your name forever and ever.

PSALMS 80–85

DAY 25

WEEK 4

HIS SALVATION IS VERY NEAR

Psalm 80

A Prayer for Restoration

FOR THE CHOIR DIRECTOR: ACCORDING TO "THE LILIES." A TESTIMONY OF ASAPH. A PSALM.

1 Listen, Shepherd of Israel,
who leads Joseph like a flock;
you who sit enthroned between the cherubim,
shine 2 on Ephraim,
Benjamin, and Manasseh.
Rally your power and come to save us.
3 Restore us, God;
make your face shine on us,
so that we may be saved.

4 LORD God of Armies,
how long will you be angry
with your people's prayers?
5 You fed them the bread of tears
and gave them a full measure
of tears to drink.
6 You put us at odds with our neighbors;
our enemies mock us.
7 Restore us, God of Armies;
make your face shine on us, so that we may be saved.

8 You dug up a vine from Egypt;
you drove out the nations and planted it.
9 You cleared a place for it;
it took root and filled the land.
10 The mountains were covered by its shade,
and the mighty cedars with its branches.
11 It sent out sprouts toward the Sea
and shoots toward the River.
12 Why have you broken down its walls
so that all who pass by pick its fruit?
13 Boars from the forest tear at it
and creatures of the field feed on it.
14 Return, God of Armies.
Look down from heaven and see;
take care of this vine,
15 the root your right hand planted,
the son that you made strong for yourself.
16 It was cut down and burned;
they perish at the rebuke of your countenance.
17 Let your hand be with the man at your right hand,
with the son of man
you have made strong for yourself.
18 Then we will not turn away from you;
revive us, and we will call on your name.
19 Restore us, LORD, God of Armies;
make your face shine on us, so that we may be saved.

Psalm 81

A Call to Obedience

FOR THE CHOIR DIRECTOR: ON THE *GITTITH*. OF ASAPH.

1 Sing for joy to God our strength;
shout in triumph to the God of Jacob.
2 Lift up a song—play the tambourine,
the melodious lyre, and the harp.
3 Blow the ram's horn on the day of our feasts
during the new moon

and during the full moon.
[4] For this is a statute for Israel,
an ordinance of the God of Jacob.
[5] He set it up as a decree for Joseph
when he went throughout the land of Egypt.
I heard an unfamiliar language:
[6] "I relieved his shoulder from the burden;
his hands were freed from carrying the basket.
[7] You called out in distress, and I rescued you;
I answered you from the thundercloud.
I tested you at the Waters of Meribah. *Selah*
[8] Listen, my people, and I will admonish you.
Israel, if you would only listen to me!
[9] There must not be a strange god among you;
you must not bow down to a foreign god.
[10] I am the Lord your God,
who brought you up from the land of Egypt.
Open your mouth wide, and I will fill it.

[11] "But my people did not listen to my voice;
Israel did not obey me.
[12] So I gave them over to their stubborn hearts
to follow their own plans.
[13] If only my people would listen to me
and Israel would follow my ways,
[14] I would quickly subdue their enemies
and turn my hand against their foes."
[15] Those who hate the Lord
would cower to him;
their doom would last forever.
[16] But he would feed Israel with the best wheat.
"I would satisfy you with honey from the rock."

Psalm 82

A Plea for Righteous Judgment
A PSALM OF ASAPH.

[1] God stands in the divine assembly;
he pronounces judgment among the gods:
[2] "How long will you judge unjustly
and show partiality to the wicked? *Selah*
[3] Provide justice for the needy and the fatherless;
uphold the rights of the oppressed and the destitute.
[4] Rescue the poor and needy;
save them from the power of the wicked."

[5] They do not know or understand;
they wander in darkness.
All the foundations of the earth are shaken.

[6] I said, "You are gods;
you are all sons of the Most High.
[7] However, you will die like humans
and fall like any other ruler."

[8] Rise up, God, judge the earth,
for all the nations belong to you.

Psalm 83

Prayer Against Enemies
A SONG. A PSALM OF ASAPH.

[1] God, do not keep silent.
Do not be deaf, God; do not be quiet.
[2] See how your enemies make an uproar;
those who hate you have acted arrogantly.
[3] They devise clever schemes against your people;
they conspire against your treasured ones.
[4] They say, "Come, let's wipe them out as a nation
so that Israel's name will no longer be remembered."
[5] For they have conspired with one mind;
they form an alliance against you—
[6] the tents of Edom and the Ishmaelites,
Moab and the Hagrites,
[7] Gebal, Ammon, and Amalek,
Philistia with the inhabitants of Tyre.
[8] Even Assyria has joined them;
they lend support to the sons of Lot. *Selah*

[9] Deal with them as you did with Midian,
as you did with Sisera
and Jabin at the Kishon River.

10 They were destroyed at En-dor;
they became manure for the ground.
11 Make their nobles like Oreb and Zeeb,
and all their tribal leaders like Zebah and Zalmunna,
12 who said, "Let's seize God's pastures for ourselves."

13 Make them like tumbleweed, my God,
like straw before the wind.
14 As fire burns a forest,
as a flame blazes through mountains,
15 so pursue them with your tempest
and terrify them with your storm.
16 Cover their faces with shame
so that they will seek your name, Lord.
17 Let them be put to shame and terrified forever;
let them perish in disgrace.
18 May they know that you alone—
whose name is the Lord—
are the Most High over the whole earth.

Psalm 84

Longing for God's House

FOR THE CHOIR DIRECTOR: ON THE *GITTITH*. A PSALM OF THE SONS OF KORAH.

1 How lovely is your dwelling place,
Lord of Armies.
2 I long and yearn
for the courts of the Lord;
my heart and flesh cry out for the living God.

3 Even a sparrow finds a home,
and a swallow, a nest for herself
where she places her young—
near your altars, Lord of Armies,
my King and my God.
4 How happy are those who reside in your house,
who praise you continually. *Selah*

5 Happy are the people whose strength is in you,
whose hearts are set on pilgrimage.

6 As they pass through the Valley of Baca,
they make it a source of spring water;
even the autumn rain will cover it with blessings.
7 They go from strength to strength;
each appears before God in Zion.

8 LORD God of Armies, hear my prayer;
listen, God of Jacob. *Selah*
9 Consider our shield, God;
look on the face of your anointed one.

10 Better a day in your courts
than a thousand anywhere else.
I would rather stand at the threshold of the house of my God
than live in the tents of wicked people.
11 For the LORD God is a sun and shield.
The LORD grants favor and honor;
he does not withhold the good
from those who live with integrity.
12 Happy is the person who trusts in you,
LORD of Armies!

Psalm 85

Restoration of Favor

FOR THE CHOIR DIRECTOR. A PSALM OF THE SONS OF KORAH.

1 LORD, you showed favor to your land;
you restored the fortunes of Jacob.
2 You forgave your people's guilt;
you covered all their sin. *Selah*
3 You withdrew all your fury;
you turned from your burning anger.

4 Return to us, God of our salvation,
and abandon your displeasure with us.
5 Will you be angry with us forever?
Will you prolong your anger for all generations?
6 Will you not revive us again
so that your people may rejoice in you?
7 Show us your faithful love, LORD,
and give us your salvation.

8 I will listen to what God will say;
surely the LORD will declare peace
to his people, his faithful ones,
and not let them go back to foolish ways.
9 His salvation is very near those who fear him,
so that glory may dwell in our land.

10 Faithful love and truth will join together;
righteousness and peace will embrace.
11 Truth will spring up from the earth,
and righteousness will look down from heaven.
12 Also, the LORD will provide what is good,
and our land will yield its crops.
13 Righteousness will go before him
to prepare the way for his steps.

Daily Response

Date:

WHAT ATTRIBUTES *of* GOD STOOD OUT TO ME?

HOW DO I CONNECT *with* THE HUMAN EXPERIENCES EXPRESSED *in* TODAY'S PSALMS?

Contextual markers	*Poetic devices or patterns*	*Words or phrases for further study*

HOW DO TODAY'S PSALMS GUIDE ME *in the* PRACTICES *of* LENT?

WHAT'S A VERSE *that* I WILL MEDITATE *on* TODAY?

Save Your Servant Who Trusts in You

PSALMS 86–89

DAY 26 .... WEEK 4

Psalm 86

Lament and Petition

A PRAYER OF DAVID.

1 Listen, LORD, and answer me,
for I am poor and needy.
2 Protect my life, for I am faithful.
You are my God; save your servant who trusts in you.
3 Be gracious to me, Lord,
for I call to you all day long.
4 Bring joy to your servant's life,
because I appeal to you, Lord.

5 For you, Lord, are kind and ready to forgive,
abounding in faithful love to all who call on you.
6 LORD, hear my prayer;
listen to my cries for mercy.
7 I call on you in the day of my distress,
for you will answer me.

8 Lord, there is no one like you among the gods,
and there are no works like yours.
9 All the nations you have made
will come and bow down before you, Lord,
and will honor your name.
10 For you are great and perform wonders;
you alone are God.

11 Teach me your way, LORD,
and I will live by your truth.
Give me an undivided mind to fear your name.
12 I will praise you with all my heart, Lord my God,
and will honor your name forever.
13 For your faithful love for me is great,
and you rescue my life from the depths of Sheol.

14 God, arrogant people have attacked me;
a gang of ruthless men intends to kill me.
They do not let you guide them.
15 But you, Lord, are a compassionate and gracious God,
slow to anger and abounding in faithful love and truth.
16 Turn to me and be gracious to me.
Give your strength to your servant;
save the son of your female servant.
17 Show me a sign of your goodness;
my enemies will see and be put to shame
because you, LORD, have helped and comforted me.

Psalm 87

Zion, the City of God

A PSALM OF THE SONS OF KORAH. A SONG.

1 The city he founded is on the holy mountains.
2 The LORD loves Zion's city gates
more than all the dwellings of Jacob.
3 Glorious things are said about you,
city of God. *Selah*

4 "I will make a record of those who know me:
Rahab, Babylon, Philistia, Tyre, and Cush—

each one was born there."
5 And it will be said of Zion,
"This one and that one were born in her."
The Most High himself will establish her.
6 When he registers the peoples,
the LORD will record,
"This one was born there." *Selah*
7 Singers and dancers alike will say,
"My whole source of joy is in you."

Psalm 88

A Cry of Desperation

A SONG. A PSALM OF THE SONS OF KORAH. FOR THE CHOIR DIRECTOR: ACCORDING TO *MAHALATH LEANNOTH*. A *MASKIL* OF HEMAN THE EZRAHITE.

1 LORD, God of my salvation,
I cry out before you day and night.
2 May my prayer reach your presence;
listen to my cry.

3 For I have had enough troubles,
and my life is near Sheol.
4 I am counted among those going down to the Pit.
I am like a man without strength,
5 abandoned among the dead.
I am like the slain lying in the grave,
whom you no longer remember,
and who are cut off from your care.

6 You have put me in the lowest part of the Pit,
in the darkest places, in the depths.
7 Your wrath weighs heavily on me;
you have overwhelmed me with all your waves. *Selah*
8 You have distanced my friends from me;
you have made me repulsive to them.
I am shut in and cannot go out.
9 My eyes are worn out from crying.
LORD, I cry out to you all day long;
I spread out my hands to you.

10 Do you work wonders for the dead?
Do departed spirits rise up to praise you? *Selah*
11 Will your faithful love be declared in the grave,
your faithfulness in Abaddon?

12 Will your wonders be known in the darkness
or your righteousness in the land of oblivion?

13 But I call to you for help, LORD;
in the morning my prayer meets you.
14 LORD, why do you reject me?
Why do you hide your face from me?
15 From my youth,
I have been suffering and near death.
I suffer your horrors; I am desperate.
16 Your wrath sweeps over me;
your terrors destroy me.
17 They surround me like water all day long;
they close in on me from every side.
18 You have distanced loved one and neighbor from me;
darkness is my only friend.

Psalm 89

Perplexity About God's Promises

A *MASKIL* OF ETHAN THE EZRAHITE.

1 I will sing about the LORD's faithful love forever;
I will proclaim your faithfulness to all generations
with my mouth.
2 For I will declare,
"Faithful love is built up forever;
you establish your faithfulness in the heavens."

3 The LORD said,
"I have made a covenant with my chosen one;
I have sworn an oath to David my servant:
4 'I will establish your offspring forever
and build up your throne for all generations.'" *Selah*

5 LORD, the heavens praise your wonders—
your faithfulness also—
in the assembly of the holy ones.
6 For who in the skies can compare with the LORD?
Who among the heavenly beings is like the LORD?
7 God is greatly feared in the council of the holy ones,
more awe-inspiring than all who surround him.
8 LORD God of Armies,
who is strong like you, LORD?
Your faithfulness surrounds you.
9 You rule the raging sea;
when its waves surge, you still them.
10 You crushed Rahab like one who is slain;
you scattered your enemies with your powerful arm.
11 The heavens are yours; the earth also is yours.
The world and everything in it—you founded them.
12 North and south—you created them.
Tabor and Hermon shout for joy at your name.
13 You have a mighty arm;
your hand is powerful;
your right hand is lifted high.
14 Righteousness and justice are the foundation
of your throne;
faithful love and truth go before you.

15 HAPPY ARE THE PEOPLE WHO
KNOW THE JOYFUL SHOUT;
LORD, THEY WALK IN THE LIGHT
FROM YOUR FACE.

16 They rejoice in your name all day long,
and they are exalted by your righteousness.
17 For you are their magnificent strength;
by your favor our horn is exalted.
18 Surely our shield belongs to the LORD,
our king to the Holy One of Israel.

19 You once spoke in a vision to your faithful ones
and said, "I have granted help to a warrior;
I have exalted one chosen from the people.
20 I have found David my servant;
I have anointed him with my sacred oil.
21 My hand will always be with him,
and my arm will strengthen him.
22 The enemy will not oppress him;
the wicked will not afflict him.
23 I will crush his foes before him
and strike those who hate him.
24 My faithfulness and love will be with him,
and through my name
his horn will be exalted.
25 I will extend his power to the sea
and his right hand to the rivers.
26 He will call to me, 'You are my Father,

my God, the rock of my salvation.'
27 I will also make him my firstborn,
greatest of the kings of the earth.
28 I will always preserve my faithful love for him,
and my covenant with him will endure.
29 I will establish his line forever,
his throne as long as heaven lasts.
30 If his sons abandon my instruction
and do not live by my ordinances,
31 if they dishonor my statutes
and do not keep my commands,
32 then I will call their rebellion
to account with the rod,
their iniquity with blows.
33 But I will not withdraw
my faithful love from him
or betray my faithfulness.
34 I will not violate my covenant
or change what my lips have said.
35 Once and for all
I have sworn an oath by my holiness;
I will not lie to David.
36 His offspring will continue forever,
his throne like the sun before me,
37 like the moon, established forever,
a faithful witness in the sky." *Selah*

38 But you have spurned and rejected him;
you have become enraged with your anointed.
39 You have repudiated the covenant with your servant;
you have completely dishonored his crown.
40 You have broken down all his walls;
you have reduced his fortified cities to ruins.
41 All who pass by plunder him;
he has become an object of ridicule
to his neighbors.
42 You have lifted high the right hand of his foes;
you have made all his enemies rejoice.
43 You have also turned back his sharp sword
and have not let him stand in battle.
44 You have made his splendor cease
and have overturned his throne.
45 You have shortened the days of his youth;
you have covered him with shame. *Selah*

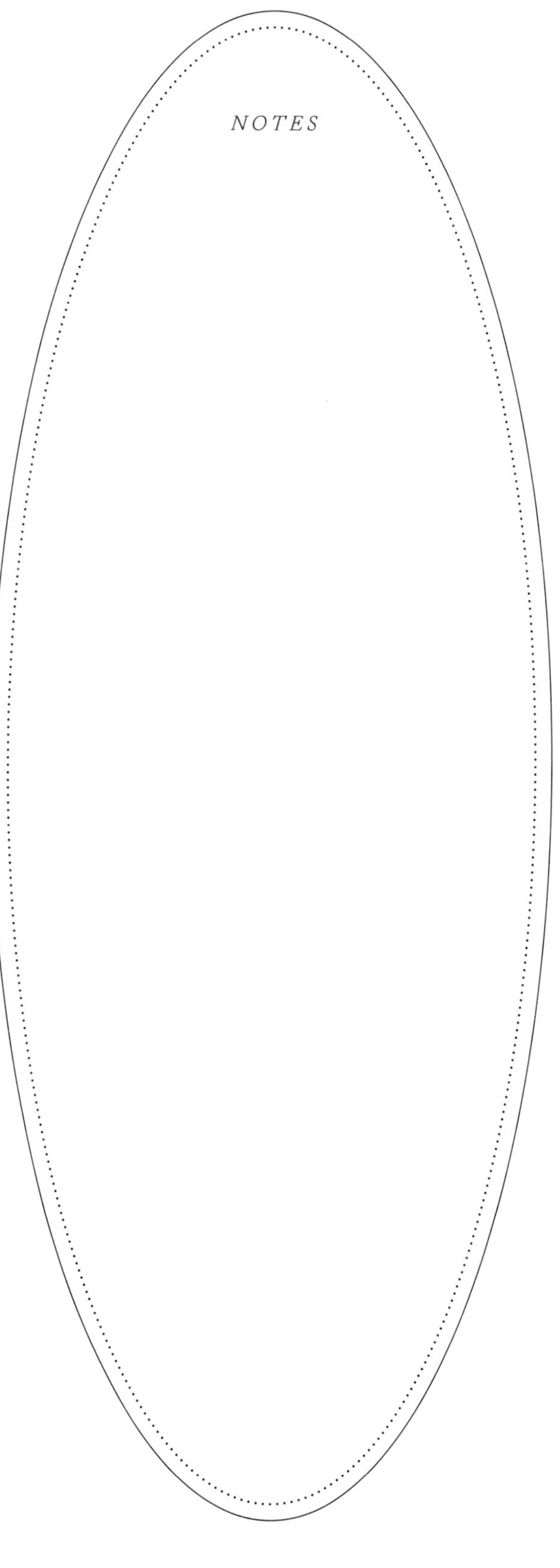

46 How long, Lord? Will you hide forever?
Will your anger keep burning like fire?
47 Remember how short my life is.
Have you created everyone for nothing?
48 What courageous person can live and never see death?
Who can save himself from the power of Sheol? *Selah*
49 Lord, where are the former acts of your faithful love
that you swore to David in your faithfulness?
50 Remember, Lord, the ridicule against your servants—
in my heart I carry abuse from all the peoples—
51 how your enemies have ridiculed, Lord,
how they have ridiculed every step of your anointed.

52 Blessed be the Lord forever.
Amen and amen.

Daily Response

Date:

WHAT ATTRIBUTES *of* GOD STOOD OUT TO ME?

HOW DO I CONNECT *with* THE HUMAN EXPERIENCES EXPRESSED *in* TODAY'S PSALMS?

Contextual markers	*Poetic devices or patterns*	*Words or phrases for further study*

HOW DO TODAY'S PSALMS GUIDE ME *in the* PRACTICES *of* LENT?

WHAT'S A VERSE *that* I WILL MEDITATE *on* TODAY?

Use Psalm 70 to respond in prayer, allowing the words of Scripture to guide your prayer. Talk to the Lord about whatever the psalm brings to mind. Refer back to the example on page 46 if you need to.

Psalm 70

A Call for Deliverance

FOR THE CHOIR DIRECTOR. OF DAVID. TO BRING REMEMBRANCE.

1 God, hurry to rescue me.
LORD, hurry to help me!

2 Let those who seek to kill me
be disgraced and confounded;
let those who wish me harm
be turned back and humiliated.

3 Let those who say, "Aha, aha!"
retreat because of their shame.

4 Let all who seek you rejoice and be glad in you;
let those who love your salvation
continually say, "God is great!"

5 I am oppressed and needy;
hurry to me, God.
You are my help and my deliverer;
LORD, do not delay.

GRACE *Day*

TAKE EACH SATURDAY *to* CATCH UP ON YOUR READING, PRAY, *and* REST *in the* PRESENCE *of the* LORD *with* PASSAGES *from* SCRIPTURE THAT WE TRADITIONALLY READ DURING *the* LENTEN SEASON.

But as it is, Christ has been raised from the dead, the firstfruits of those who have fallen asleep. For since death came through a man, the resurrection of the dead also comes through a man. For just as in Adam all die, so also in Christ all will be made alive.

1 CORINTHIANS 15:20–22

DAY 28 - WEEK 4

WEEKLY TRUTH

SCRIPTURE IS GOD BREATHED *and* TRUE.
WHEN WE MEMORIZE IT, WE CARRY HIS WORD
with US WHEREVER WE GO.

EACH SUNDAY DURING THIS PLAN, WE ARE
READING *a* DIFFERENT HALLEL PSALM *and*
MEMORIZING ONE *of* ITS VERSES.

THIS WEEK, MEMORIZE PSALM 116:13 AS YOU
MEDITATE *on the* PSALM *as a* WHOLE.

Psalm 116

Thanks to God for Deliverance

1 I love the LORD because he has heard
my appeal for mercy.
2 Because he has turned his ear to me,
I will call out to him as long as I live.

3 The ropes of death were wrapped around me,
and the torments of Sheol overcame me;
I encountered trouble and sorrow.
4 Then I called on the name of the LORD:
"LORD, save me!"

5 The LORD is gracious and righteous;
our God is compassionate.
6 The LORD guards the inexperienced;
I was helpless, and he saved me.
7 Return to your rest, my soul,
for the LORD has been good to you.
8 For you, LORD, rescued me from death,
my eyes from tears,
my feet from stumbling.
9 I will walk before the LORD
in the land of the living.
10 I believed, even when I said,
"I am severely oppressed."
11 In my alarm I said,
"Everyone is a liar."

12 How can I repay the LORD
for all the good he has done for me?
13 I will take the cup of salvation
and call on the name of the LORD.
14 I will fulfill my vows to the LORD
in the presence of all his people.

15 The death of his faithful ones
is valuable in the LORD's sight.
16 LORD, I am indeed your servant;
I am your servant, the son of your
female servant.
You have loosened my bonds.

17 I will offer you a thanksgiving sacrifice
and call on the name of the LORD.
18 I will fulfill my vows to the LORD
in the presence of all his people,
19 in the courts of the LORD's house—
within you, Jerusalem.
Hallelujah!

SEE TIPS FOR MEMORIZING SCRIPTURE ON PAGE 272.

PSALMS 90–95

GIVE THANKS *to the* LORD

It is good to give thanks to the LORD, to sing praise to your name, Most High.

Psalm 92:1

Psalm 90

Eternal God and Mortal Man

A PRAYER OF MOSES, THE MAN OF GOD.

1 Lord, you have been our refuge
in every generation.
2 Before the mountains were born,
before you gave birth to the earth and the world,
from eternity to eternity, you are God.

3 You return mankind to the dust,
saying, "Return, descendants of Adam."
4 For in your sight a thousand years
are like yesterday that passes by,
like a few hours of the night.
5 You end their lives; they sleep.
They are like grass that grows in the morning—
6 in the morning it sprouts and grows;
by evening it withers and dries up.

7 For we are consumed by your anger;
we are terrified by your wrath.
8 You have set our iniquities before you,
our secret sins in the light of your presence.
9 For all our days ebb away under your wrath;
we end our years like a sigh.
10 Our lives last seventy years
or, if we are strong, eighty years.
Even the best of them are struggle and sorrow;
indeed, they pass quickly and we fly away.
11 Who understands the power of your anger?
Your wrath matches the fear that is due you.
12 Teach us to number our days carefully
so that we may develop wisdom in our hearts.

13 Lord—how long?
Turn and have compassion on your servants.
14 Satisfy us in the morning with your faithful love
so that we may shout with joy and be glad all our days.
15 Make us rejoice for as many days as you have humbled us,
for as many years as we have seen adversity.
16 Let your work be seen by your servants,
and your splendor by their children.
17 Let the favor of the Lord our God be on us;
establish for us the work of our hands—
establish the work of our hands!

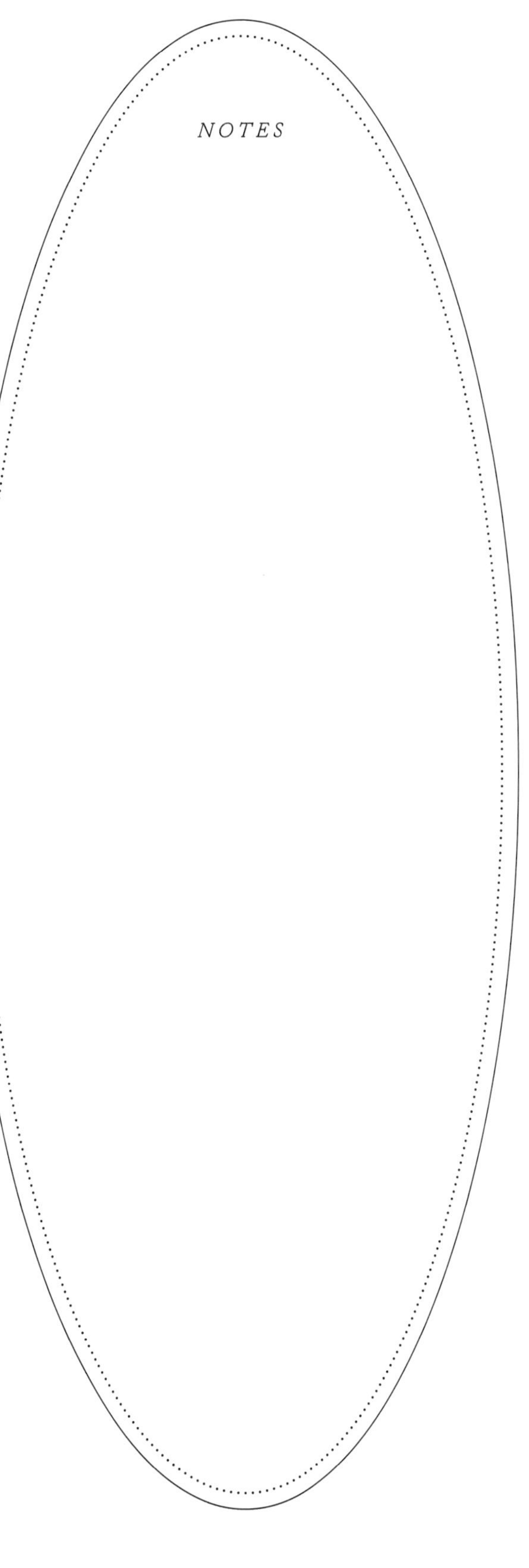

Psalm 91

The Protection of the Most High

[1] The one who lives under the protection of the Most High
dwells in the shadow of the Almighty.

[2] I will say concerning the LORD, who is my refuge
and my fortress,
my God in whom I trust:
[3] He himself will rescue you from the bird trap,
from the destructive plague.
[4] He will cover you with his feathers;
you will take refuge under his wings.
His faithfulness will be a protective shield.
[5] You will not fear the terror of the night,
the arrow that flies by day,
[6] the plague that stalks in darkness,
or the pestilence that ravages at noon.
[7] Though a thousand fall at your side
and ten thousand at your right hand,
the pestilence will not reach you.
[8] You will only see it with your eyes
and witness the punishment of the wicked.

[9] Because you have made the LORD—my refuge,
the Most High—your dwelling place,
[10] no harm will come to you;
no plague will come near your tent.
[11] For he will give his angels orders concerning you,
to protect you in all your ways.
[12] They will support you with their hands
so that you will not strike your foot against a stone.
[13] You will tread on the lion and the cobra;
you will trample the young lion and the serpent.

[14] Because he has his heart set on me,
I will deliver him;
I will protect him because he knows my name.
[15] When he calls out to me, I will answer him;
I will be with him in trouble.
I will rescue him and give him honor.
[16] I will satisfy him with a long life
and show him my salvation.

Psalm 92

God's Love and Faithfulness

A PSALM. A SONG FOR THE SABBATH DAY.

[1] It is good to give thanks to the LORD,
to sing praise to your name, Most High,
[2] to declare your faithful love in the morning
and your faithfulness at night,
[3] with a ten-stringed harp
and the music of a lyre.

[4] For you have made me rejoice, LORD,
by what you have done;
I will shout for joy
because of the works of your hands.
[5] How magnificent are your works, LORD,
how profound your thoughts!
[6] A stupid person does not know,
a fool does not understand this:
[7] though the wicked sprout like grass
and all evildoers flourish,
they will be eternally destroyed.
[8] But you, LORD, are exalted forever.
[9] For indeed, LORD, your enemies—
indeed, your enemies will perish;
all evildoers will be scattered.
[10] You have lifted up my horn
like that of a wild ox;
I have been anointed with the finest oil.
[11] My eyes look at my enemies;
when evildoers rise against me,
my ears hear them.

[12] The righteous thrive like a palm tree
and grow like a cedar tree in Lebanon.
[13] Planted in the house of the LORD,
they thrive in the courts of our God.
[14] They will still bear fruit in old age,
healthy and green,
[15] to declare, "The LORD is just;
he is my rock,
and there is no unrighteousness in him."

Psalm 93

God's Eternal Reign

1 The LORD reigns! He is robed in majesty;
the LORD is robed, enveloped in strength.
The world is firmly established;
it cannot be shaken.
2 Your throne has been established
from the beginning;
you are from eternity.
3 The floods have lifted up, LORD,
the floods have lifted up their voice;
the floods lift up their pounding waves.
4 Greater than the roar of a huge torrent—
the mighty breakers of the sea—
the LORD on high is majestic.

5 LORD, your testimonies are completely reliable;
holiness adorns your house
for all the days to come.

NOTES

Psalm 94

The Just Judge

1 LORD, God of vengeance—
God of vengeance, shine!
2 Rise up, Judge of the earth;
repay the proud what they deserve.
3 LORD, how long will the wicked—
how long will the wicked celebrate?

4 They pour out arrogant words;
all the evildoers boast.
5 LORD, they crush your people;
they oppress your heritage.
6 They kill the widow and the resident alien
and murder the fatherless.
7 They say, "The LORD doesn't see it.
The God of Jacob doesn't pay attention."

8 Pay attention, you stupid people!
Fools, when will you be wise?

[9] Can the one who shaped the ear not hear,
the one who formed the eye not see?
[10] The one who instructs nations,
the one who teaches mankind knowledge—
does he not discipline?
[11] The LORD knows the thoughts of mankind;
they are futile.

[12] LORD, how happy is anyone you discipline
and teach from your law
[13] to give him relief from troubled times
until a pit is dug for the wicked.
[14] The LORD will not leave his people
or abandon his heritage,
[15] for the administration of justice will again be righteous,
and all the upright in heart will follow it.

[16] Who stands up for me against the wicked?
Who takes a stand for me against evildoers?
[17] If the LORD had not been my helper,
I would soon rest in the silence of death.
[18] If I say, "My foot is slipping,"
your faithful love will support me, LORD.
[19] When I am filled with cares,
your comfort brings me joy.

[20] Can a corrupt throne be your ally,
a throne that makes evil laws?
[21] They band together against the life of the righteous
and condemn the innocent to death.
[22] But the LORD is my refuge;
my God is the rock of my protection.
[23] He will pay them back for their sins
and destroy them for their evil.
The LORD our God will destroy them.

Psalm 95

Worship and Warning

[1] Come, let's shout joyfully to the LORD,
shout triumphantly to the rock of our salvation!
[2] Let's enter his presence with thanksgiving;
let's shout triumphantly to him in song.

[3] For the LORD is a great God,
a great King above all gods.
[4] The depths of the earth are in his hand,
and the mountain peaks are his.
[5] The sea is his; he made it.
His hands formed the dry land.

[6] Come, let's worship and bow down;
let's kneel before the LORD our Maker.

[7] FOR HE IS OUR GOD,
AND WE ARE THE PEOPLE OF
HIS PASTURE,
THE SHEEP UNDER HIS CARE.

Today, if you hear his voice:
[8] Do not harden your hearts as at Meribah,
as on that day at Massah in the wilderness
[9] where your ancestors tested me;
they tried me, though they had seen what I did.
[10] For forty years I was disgusted with that generation;
I said, "They are a people whose hearts go astray;
they do not know my ways."
[11] So I swore in my anger,
"They will not enter my rest."

Daily Response

Date:

WHAT ATTRIBUTES *of* GOD STOOD OUT TO ME?

HOW DO I CONNECT *with* THE HUMAN EXPERIENCES EXPRESSED *in* TODAY'S PSALMS?

Contextual markers

Poetic devices or patterns

Words or phrases for further study

HOW DO TODAY'S PSALMS GUIDE ME *in the* PRACTICES *of* LENT?

WHAT'S A VERSE *that* I WILL MEDITATE *on* TODAY?

DAY 30

Psalms 96–102

PROCLAIM HIS SALVATION

Psalm 96

King of the Earth

1 Sing a new song to the LORD;
let the whole earth sing to the LORD.
2 Sing to the LORD, bless his name;
proclaim his salvation from day to day.
3 Declare his glory among the nations,
his wondrous works among all peoples.

4 For the LORD is great and is highly praised;
he is feared above all gods.
5 For all the gods of the peoples are worthless idols,
but the LORD made the heavens.
6 Splendor and majesty are before him;
strength and beauty are in his sanctuary.

7 Ascribe to the LORD, you families of the peoples,
ascribe to the LORD glory and strength.
8 Ascribe to the LORD the glory of his name;
bring an offering and enter his courts.
9 Worship the LORD in the splendor of his holiness;
let the whole earth tremble before him.

10 Say among the nations, "The LORD reigns.
The world is firmly established; it cannot be shaken.
He judges the peoples fairly."
11 Let the heavens be glad and the earth rejoice;
let the sea and all that fills it resound.
12 Let the fields and everything in them celebrate.
Then all the trees of the forest will shout for joy
13 before the LORD, for he is coming—
for he is coming to judge the earth.
He will judge the world with righteousness
and the peoples with his faithfulness.

Psalm 97

The Majestic King

1 The LORD reigns! Let the earth rejoice;
let the many coasts and islands be glad.

2 Clouds and total darkness surround him;
righteousness and justice are the foundation of his throne.

NOTES

3 Fire goes before him
and burns up his foes on every side.
4 His lightning lights up the world;
the earth sees and trembles.
5 The mountains melt like wax
at the presence of the LORD—
at the presence of the Lord of the whole earth.

6 The heavens proclaim his righteousness;
all the peoples see his glory.

7 All who serve carved images,
those who boast in worthless idols, will be put to shame.
All the gods must worship him.

8 Zion hears and is glad,
Judah's villages rejoice
because of your judgments, LORD.
9 For you, LORD,
are the Most High over the whole earth;
you are exalted above all the gods.

10 You who love the LORD, hate evil!
He protects the lives of his faithful ones;
he rescues them from the power of the wicked.
11 Light dawns for the righteous,
gladness for the upright in heart.
12 Be glad in the LORD, you righteous ones,
and give thanks to his holy name.

Psalm 98

Praise the King

A PSALM.

1 Sing a new song to the LORD,
for he has performed wonders;
his right hand and holy arm
have won him victory.
2 The LORD has made his victory known;
he has revealed his righteousness
in the sight of the nations.
3 He has remembered his love
and faithfulness to the house of Israel;
all the ends of the earth
have seen our God's victory.

4 Let the whole earth shout to the LORD;
be jubilant, shout for joy, and sing.
5 Sing to the LORD with the lyre,
with the lyre and melodious song.
6 With trumpets and the blast of the ram's horn
shout triumphantly
in the presence of the LORD, our King.

7 Let the sea and all that fills it,
the world and those who live in it, resound.
8 Let the rivers clap their hands;
let the mountains shout together for joy
9 before the LORD,
for he is coming to judge the earth.
He will judge the world righteously
and the peoples fairly.

Psalm 99

The King Is Holy

1 The LORD reigns! Let the peoples tremble.
He is enthroned between the cherubim.
Let the earth quake.
2 The LORD is great in Zion;
he is exalted above all the peoples.
3 Let them praise your great
and awe-inspiring name.
He is holy.

4 The mighty King loves justice.
You have established fairness;
you have administered justice
and righteousness in Jacob.
5 Exalt the LORD our God;
bow in worship at his footstool.
He is holy.

6 Moses and Aaron were among his priests;
Samuel also was among those calling on his name.
They called to the LORD and he answered them.

7 He spoke to them in a pillar of cloud;
they kept his decrees and the statutes he gave them.
8 LORD our God, you answered them.
You were a forgiving God to them,
but an avenger of their sinful actions.

9 Exalt the LORD our God;
bow in worship at his holy mountain,
for the LORD our God is holy.

Psalm 100

Be Thankful

A PSALM OF THANKSGIVING.

1 Let the whole earth shout triumphantly to the LORD!
2 Serve the LORD with gladness;
come before him with joyful songs.
3 Acknowledge that the LORD is God.
He made us, and we are his—
his people, the sheep of his pasture.
4 Enter his gates with thanksgiving
and his courts with praise.
Give thanks to him and bless his name.
5 For the LORD is good, and his faithful love endures forever;
his faithfulness, through all generations.

Psalm 101

A Vow of Integrity

A PSALM OF DAVID.

1 I will sing of faithful love and justice;
I will sing praise to you, LORD.
2 I will pay attention to the way of integrity.
When will you come to me?
I will live with a heart of integrity in my house.
3 I will not let anything worthless guide me.
I hate the practice of transgression;
it will not cling to me.
4 A devious heart will be far from me;
I will not be involved with evil.

5 I will destroy anyone
who secretly slanders his neighbor;

I cannot tolerate anyone
with haughty eyes or an arrogant heart.
[6] My eyes favor the faithful of the land
so that they may sit down with me.
The one who follows the way of integrity
may serve me.
[7] No one who acts deceitfully
will live in my palace;
the one who tells lies
will not be retained here to guide me.
[8] Every morning I will destroy
all the wicked of the land,
wiping out all evildoers from the LORD's city.

Psalm 102

Affliction in Light of Eternity

A PRAYER OF A SUFFERING PERSON WHO IS WEAK AND POURS OUT HIS LAMENT BEFORE THE LORD.

[1] LORD, hear my prayer;
let my cry for help come before you.
[2] Do not hide your face from me in my day of trouble.
Listen closely to me;
answer me quickly when I call.

[3] For my days vanish like smoke,
and my bones burn like a furnace.
[4] My heart is suffering, withered like grass;
I even forget to eat my food.
[5] Because of the sound of my groaning,
my flesh sticks to my bones.
[6] I am like an eagle owl,
like a little owl among the ruins.
[7] I stay awake;
I am like a solitary bird on a roof.
[8] My enemies taunt me all day long;
they ridicule and use my name as a curse.
[9] I eat ashes like bread
and mingle my drinks with tears
[10] because of your indignation and wrath;
for you have picked me up and thrown me aside.
[11] My days are like a lengthening shadow,
and I wither away like grass.

[12] But you, LORD, are enthroned forever;
your fame endures to all generations.
[13] You will rise up and have compassion on Zion,
for it is time to show favor to her—
the appointed time has come.
[14] For your servants take delight in its stones
and favor its dust.

[15] Then the nations will fear the name of the LORD,
and all the kings of the earth your glory,
[16] for the LORD will rebuild Zion;
he will appear in his glory.
[17] He will pay attention to the prayer of the destitute
and will not despise their prayer.

[18] This will be written for a later generation,
and a people who have not yet been created will
praise the LORD:
[19] He looked down from his holy heights—
the LORD gazed out from heaven to earth—
[20] to hear a prisoner's groaning,
to set free those condemned to die,
[21] so that they might declare
the name of the LORD in Zion
and his praise in Jerusalem
[22] when peoples and kingdoms are assembled
to serve the LORD.

[23] He has broken my strength in midcourse;
he has shortened my days.
[24] I say, "My God, do not take me
in the middle of my life!
Your years continue through all generations.
[25] Long ago you established the earth,
and the heavens are the work of your hands.
[26] They will perish, but you will endure;
all of them will wear out like clothing.
You will change them like a garment,
and they will pass away.
[27] But you are the same,
and your years will never end.
[28] Your servants' children will dwell securely,
and their offspring will be established before you."

Daily Response

Date:

WHAT ATTRIBUTES *of* GOD STOOD OUT TO ME?

HOW DO I CONNECT *with* THE HUMAN EXPERIENCES EXPRESSED *in* TODAY'S PSALMS?

Contextual markers

Poetic devices or patterns

Words or phrases for further study

HOW DO TODAY'S PSALMS GUIDE ME *in the* PRACTICES *of* LENT?

WHAT'S A VERSE *that* I WILL MEDITATE *on* TODAY?

MY SOUL, BLESS *the* LORD

Psalms 103–105

DAY
31

WEEK
5

Psalm 103

The Forgiving God

OF DAVID.

1 My soul, bless the LORD,
and all that is within me, bless his holy name.
2 My soul, bless the LORD,
and do not forget all his benefits.

3 He forgives all your iniquity;
he heals all your diseases.
4 He redeems your life from the Pit;
he crowns you with faithful love and compassion.
5 He satisfies you with good things;
your youth is renewed like the eagle.

6 The LORD executes acts of righteousness
and justice for all the oppressed.
7 He revealed his ways to Moses,
his deeds to the people of Israel.
8 The LORD is compassionate and gracious,
slow to anger and abounding in faithful love.
9 He will not always accuse us
or be angry forever.
10 He has not dealt with us as our sins deserve
or repaid us according to our iniquities.

11 For as high as the heavens are above the earth,
so great is his faithful love
toward those who fear him.
12 As far as the east is from the west,
so far has he removed
our transgressions from us.
13 As a father has compassion on his children,
so the LORD has compassion on those who fear him.
14 For he knows what we are made of,
remembering that we are dust.

15 As for man, his days are like grass—
he blooms like a flower of the field;
16 when the wind passes over it, it vanishes,
and its place is no longer known.
17 But from eternity to eternity
the LORD's faithful love is toward those who fear him,
and his righteousness toward the grandchildren

[18] of those who keep his covenant,
who remember to observe his precepts.
[19] The LORD has established his throne in heaven,
and his kingdom rules over all.

[20] Bless the LORD,
all his angels of great strength,
who do his word,
obedient to his command.
[21] Bless the LORD, all his armies,
his servants who do his will.
[22] Bless the LORD, all his works
in all the places where he rules.
My soul, bless the LORD!

Psalm 104

God the Creator

[1] My soul, bless the LORD!
LORD my God, you are very great;
you are clothed with majesty and splendor.
[2] He wraps himself in light as if it were a robe,
spreading out the sky like a canopy,
[3] laying the beams of his palace
on the waters above,
making the clouds his chariot,
walking on the wings of the wind,
[4] and making the winds his messengers,
flames of fire his servants.

[5] He established the earth on its foundations;
it will never be shaken.
[6] You covered it with the deep
as if it were a garment;
the water stood above the mountains.
[7] At your rebuke the water fled;
at the sound of your thunder they hurried away—
[8] mountains rose and valleys sank—
to the place you established for them.
[9] You set a boundary they cannot cross;
they will never cover the earth again.

[10] He causes the springs to gush into the valleys;
they flow between the mountains.
[11] They supply water for every wild beast;
the wild donkeys quench their thirst.
[12] The birds of the sky live beside the springs;
they make their voices heard among the foliage.
[13] He waters the mountains from his palace;
the earth is satisfied by the fruit of your labor.

[14] He causes grass to grow for the livestock
and provides crops for man to cultivate,
producing food from the earth,
[15] wine that makes human hearts glad—
making his face shine with oil—
and bread that sustains human hearts.

[16] The trees of the LORD flourish,
the cedars of Lebanon that he planted.
[17] There the birds make their nests;
storks make their homes in the pine trees.
[18] The high mountains are for the wild goats;
the cliffs are a refuge for hyraxes.

[19] He made the moon to mark the festivals;
the sun knows when to set.
[20] You bring darkness, and it becomes night,
when all the forest animals stir.
[21] The young lions roar for their prey
and seek their food from God.
[22] The sun rises; they go back
and lie down in their dens.
[23] Man goes out to his work
and to his labor until evening.

[24] How countless are your works, LORD!
In wisdom you have made them all;
the earth is full of your creatures.
[25] Here is the sea, vast and wide,
teeming with creatures beyond number—
living things both large and small.
[26] There the ships move about,
and Leviathan, which you formed to play there.

[27] All of them wait for you
to give them their food at the right time.
[28] When you give it to them,

they gather it;
when you open your hand,
they are satisfied with good things.
29 When you hide your face,
they are terrified;
when you take away their breath,
they die and return to the dust.
30 When you send your breath,
they are created,
and you renew the surface of the ground.

31 May the glory of the LORD endure forever;
may the LORD rejoice in his works.
32 He looks at the earth, and it trembles;
he touches the mountains,
and they pour out smoke.
33 I will sing to the LORD all my life;
I will sing praise to my God while I live.
34 May my meditation be pleasing to him;
I will rejoice in the LORD.
35 May sinners vanish from the earth
and wicked people be no more.
My soul, bless the LORD!
Hallelujah!

Psalm 105

God's Faithfulness to His People

1 Give thanks to the LORD, call on his name;
proclaim his deeds among the peoples.
2 Sing to him, sing praise to him;
tell about all his wondrous works!
3 Boast in his holy name;
let the hearts of those who seek the LORD rejoice.
4 Seek the LORD and his strength;
seek his face always.
5 Remember the wondrous works he has done,
his wonders, and the judgments he has pronounced,
6 you offspring of Abraham his servant,
Jacob's descendants—his chosen ones.

7 He is the LORD our God;
his judgments govern the whole earth.

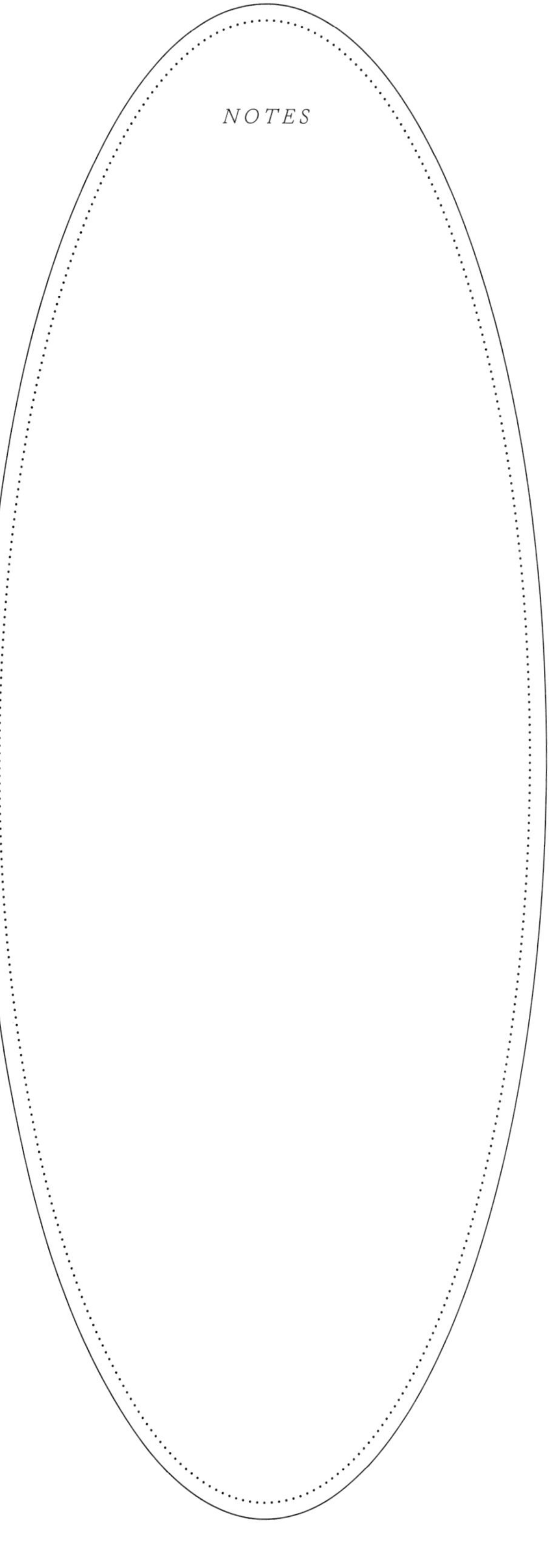

[8] He remembers his covenant forever,
the promise he ordained
for a thousand generations—
[9] the covenant he made with Abraham,
swore to Isaac,
[10] and confirmed to Jacob as a decree
and to Israel as a permanent covenant:
[11] "I will give the land of Canaan to you
as your inherited portion."

[12] When they were few in number,
very few indeed,
and resident aliens in Canaan,
[13] wandering from nation to nation
and from one kingdom to another,
[14] he allowed no one to oppress them;
he rebuked kings on their behalf:
[15] "Do not touch my anointed ones,
or harm my prophets."

[16] He called down famine against the land
and destroyed the entire food supply.
[17] He had sent a man ahead of them—
Joseph, who was sold as a slave.
[18] They hurt his feet with shackles;
his neck was put in an iron collar.
[19] Until the time his prediction came true,
the word of the Lord tested him.
[20] The king sent for him and released him;
the ruler of peoples set him free.
[21] He made him master of his household,
ruler over all his possessions—
[22] binding his officials at will
and instructing his elders.

[23] Then Israel went to Egypt;
Jacob lived as an alien in the land of Ham.
[24] The Lord made his people very fruitful;
he made them more numerous than their foes,
[25] whose hearts he turned to hate his people
and to deal deceptively with his servants.
[26] He sent Moses his servant,
and Aaron, whom he had chosen.
[27] They performed his miraculous signs among them
and wonders in the land of Ham.
[28] He sent darkness, and it became dark—
for did they not defy his commands?
[29] He turned their water into blood
and caused their fish to die.
[30] Their land was overrun with frogs,
even in their royal chambers.
[31] He spoke, and insects came—
gnats throughout their country.
[32] He gave them hail for rain,
and lightning throughout their land.
[33] He struck their vines and fig trees
and shattered the trees of their territory.
[34] He spoke, and locusts came—
young locusts without number.
[35] They devoured all the vegetation in their land
and consumed the produce of their land.
[36] He struck all the firstborn in their land,
all their first progeny.

[37] Then he brought Israel out with silver and gold,
and no one among his tribes stumbled.
[38] Egypt was glad when they left,
for the dread of Israel had fallen on them.
[39] He spread a cloud as a covering
and gave a fire to light up the night.
[40] They asked, and he brought quail
and satisfied them with bread from heaven.
[41] He opened a rock, and water gushed out;
it flowed like a stream in the desert.
[42] For he remembered his holy promise
to Abraham his servant.
[43] He brought his people out with rejoicing,
his chosen ones with shouts of joy.
[44] He gave them the lands of the nations,
and they inherited
what other peoples had worked for.

[45] All this happened
so that they might keep his statutes
and obey his instructions.
Hallelujah!

Daily Response

Date:

WHAT ATTRIBUTES *of* GOD STOOD OUT TO ME?

HOW DO I CONNECT *with* THE HUMAN EXPERIENCES EXPRESSED *in* TODAY'S PSALMS?

Contextual markers

Poetic devices or patterns

Words or phrases for further study

HOW DO TODAY'S PSALMS GUIDE ME *in the* PRACTICES *of* LENT?

WHAT'S A VERSE *that* I WILL MEDITATE *on* TODAY?

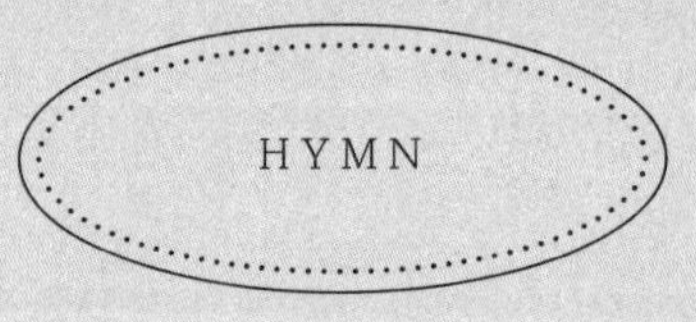

PRAISE TO THE LORD, THE ALMIGHTY

WORDS

German Hymn, Joachim Neander; translated by Catherine Winkworth

MUSIC

Stralsund Gesangbuch; *harmony by W. Sterndale Bennett; last stanza setting by Bruce Greer*

1. Praise to the Lord, the Al - might - y, the King of cre - a - tion! O my soul, praise Him, for He is thy health and sal - va - tion! All ye who hear, Now to His tem - ple draw near; Praise Him in glad ad - o - ra - tion!
2. Praise to the Lord, who o'er all things so won - drous - ly reign - eth, Shel - ters thee un - der His wings, yea, so gen - tly sus - tain - eth! Hast thou not seen How thy de - sires e'er have been Grant - ed in what He or - dain - eth?
3. Praise to the Lord, who doth pros - per thy work and de - fend thee; Sure - ly His good - ness and mer - cy here dai - ly at - tend thee. Pon - der a - new What the Al - might - y can do If with His love He be - friend thee.
4. Praise to the Lord, O let all that is in me a - dore Him! All that hath life and breath, come now with prais - es be - fore Him. Let the A - men Sound from His peo - ple a - gain; Glad - ly for aye we a - dore Him!

Consider the Lord's Acts

PSALMS 106–107

DAY 32 ····················· WEEK 5

Psalm 106

Israel's Unfaithfulness to God

1 Hallelujah!
Give thanks to the Lord, for he is good;
his faithful love endures forever.
2 Who can declare the Lord's mighty acts
or proclaim all the praise due him?
3 How happy are those who uphold justice,
who practice righteousness at all times.

4 Remember me, Lord,
when you show favor to your people.
Come to me with your salvation
5 so that I may enjoy the prosperity
of your chosen ones,
rejoice in the joy of your nation,
and boast about your heritage.

6 Both we and our ancestors have sinned;
we have done wrong and have acted wickedly.
7 Our ancestors in Egypt did not grasp
the significance of your wondrous works
or remember your many acts of faithful love;
instead, they rebelled by the sea—the Red Sea.
8 Yet he saved them for his name's sake,
to make his power known.
9 He rebuked the Red Sea, and it dried up;
he led them through the depths as through a desert.
10 He saved them from the power of the adversary;
he redeemed them from the power of the enemy.
11 Water covered their foes;
not one of them remained.
12 Then they believed his promises
and sang his praise.

13 They soon forgot his works
and would not wait for his counsel.
14 They were seized with craving in the wilderness
and tested God in the desert.
15 He gave them what they asked for,
but sent a wasting disease among them.

16 In the camp they were envious of Moses
and of Aaron, the Lord's holy one.
17 The earth opened up and swallowed Dathan;
it covered the assembly of Abiram.
18 Fire blazed throughout their assembly;
flames consumed the wicked.

19 At Horeb they made a calf
and worshiped the cast metal image.
20 They exchanged their glory
for the image of a grass-eating ox.
21 They forgot God their Savior,
who did great things in Egypt,
22 wondrous works in the land of Ham,

awe-inspiring acts at the Red Sea.
23 So he said he would have destroyed them—
if Moses his chosen one
had not stood before him in the breach
to turn his wrath away from destroying them.

24 They despised the pleasant land
and did not believe his promise.
25 They grumbled in their tents
and did not listen to the LORD.
26 So he raised his hand against them with an oath
that he would make them fall in the desert
27 and would disperse their descendants
among the nations,
scattering them throughout the lands.

28 They aligned themselves with Baal of Peor
and ate sacrifices offered to lifeless gods.
29 They angered the LORD with their deeds,
and a plague broke out against them.
30 But Phinehas stood up and intervened,
and the plague was stopped.
31 It was credited to him as righteousness
throughout all generations to come.

32 They angered the LORD at the Waters of Meribah,
and Moses suffered because of them,
33 for they embittered his spirit,
and he spoke rashly with his lips.

34 They did not destroy the peoples
as the LORD had commanded them
35 but mingled with the nations
and adopted their ways.
36 They served their idols,
which became a snare to them.
37 They sacrificed their sons and daughters to demons.
38 They shed innocent blood—
the blood of their sons and daughters
whom they sacrificed to the idols of Canaan;
so the land became polluted with blood.
39 They defiled themselves by their actions
and prostituted themselves by their deeds.

40 Therefore the LORD's anger burned against his people,
and he abhorred his own inheritance.
41 He handed them over to the nations;
those who hated them ruled over them.
42 Their enemies oppressed them,
and they were subdued under their power.
43 He rescued them many times,
but they continued to rebel deliberately
and were beaten down by their iniquity.

44 When he heard their cry,
he took note of their distress,
45 remembered his covenant with them,
and relented according to the abundance
of his faithful love.
46 He caused them to be pitied
before all their captors.

47 Save us, LORD our God,
and gather us from the nations,
so that we may give thanks to your holy name
and rejoice in your praise.

48 Blessed be the LORD God of Israel,
from everlasting to everlasting.
Let all the people say, "Amen!"
Hallelujah!

Psalm 107

Thanksgiving for God's Deliverance

1 Give thanks to the LORD, for he is good;
his faithful love endures forever.
2 Let the redeemed of the LORD proclaim
that he has redeemed them from the power of the foe
3 and has gathered them from the lands—
from the east and the west,
from the north and the south.

4 Some wandered in the desolate wilderness,
finding no way to a city where they could live.
5 They were hungry and thirsty;
their spirits failed within them.

6 Then they cried out to the LORD in their trouble;
he rescued them from their distress.
7 He led them by the right path
to go to a city where they could live.
8 Let them give thanks to the LORD
for his faithful love
and his wondrous works for all humanity.
9 For he has satisfied the thirsty
and filled the hungry with good things.

10 Others sat in darkness and gloom—
prisoners in cruel chains—
11 because they rebelled against God's commands
and despised the counsel of the Most High.
12 He broke their spirits with hard labor;
they stumbled, and there was no one to help.
13 Then they cried out to the LORD in their trouble;
he saved them from their distress.
14 He brought them out of darkness and gloom
and broke their chains apart.
15 Let them give thanks to the LORD
for his faithful love
and his wondrous works for all humanity.
16 For he has broken down the bronze gates
and cut through the iron bars.

17 Fools suffered affliction
because of their rebellious ways and their iniquities.
18 They loathed all food
and came near the gates of death.
19 Then they cried out to the LORD in their trouble;
he saved them from their distress.
20 He sent his word and healed them;
he rescued them from their traps.
21 Let them give thanks to the LORD
for his faithful love
and his wondrous works for all humanity.
22 Let them offer thanksgiving sacrifices
and announce his works with shouts of joy.

23 Others went to sea in ships,
conducting trade on the vast water.
24 They saw the LORD's works,
his wondrous works in the deep.
25 He spoke and raised a stormy wind
that stirred up the waves of the sea.
26 Rising up to the sky, sinking down to the depths,
their courage melting away in anguish,
27 they reeled and staggered like a drunkard,
and all their skill was useless.
28 Then they cried out to the LORD in their trouble,
and he brought them out of their distress.
29 He stilled the storm to a whisper,
and the waves of the sea were hushed.
30 They rejoiced when the waves grew quiet.
Then he guided them to the harbor they longed for.
31 Let them give thanks to the LORD
for his faithful love
and his wondrous works for all humanity.
32 Let them exalt him in the assembly of the people
and praise him in the council of the elders.

33 He turns rivers into desert,
springs into thirsty ground,
34 and fruitful land into salty wasteland,
because of the wickedness of its inhabitants.
35 He turns a desert into a pool,
dry land into springs.
36 He causes the hungry to settle there,
and they establish a city where they can live.
37 They sow fields and plant vineyards
that yield a fruitful harvest.
38 He blesses them, and they multiply greatly;
he does not let their livestock decrease.

39 When they are diminished and are humbled
by cruel oppression and sorrow,
40 he pours contempt on nobles
and makes them wander in a trackless wasteland.
41 But he lifts the needy out of their suffering
and makes their families multiply like flocks.
42 The upright see it and rejoice,
and all injustice shuts its mouth.

43 Let whoever is wise pay attention to these things
and consider the LORD's acts of faithful love.

Daily Response

Date:

WHAT ATTRIBUTES *of* GOD STOOD OUT TO ME?

HOW DO I CONNECT *with* THE HUMAN EXPERIENCES EXPRESSED *in* TODAY'S PSALMS?

Contextual markers

Poetic devices or patterns

Words or phrases for further study

HOW DO TODAY'S PSALMS GUIDE ME *in the* PRACTICES *of* LENT?

WHAT'S A VERSE *that* I WILL MEDITATE *on* TODAY?

HE HAS SENT REDEMPTION

Psalms 108–112

HE HAS SENT REDEMPTION *to* HIS PEOPLE. HE HAS ORDAINED HIS COVENANT FOREVER. HIS NAME IS HOLY *and* AWE-INSPIRING.

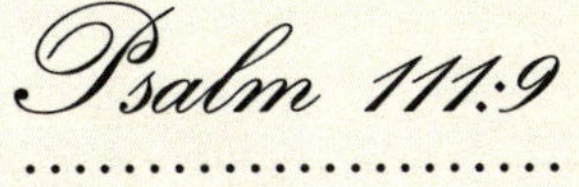

DAY
33

WEEK
5

Psalm 108

A Plea for Victory

A SONG. A PSALM OF DAVID.

1 My heart is confident, God;
I will sing; I will sing praises
with the whole of my being.
2 Wake up, harp and lyre!
I will wake up the dawn.
3 I will praise you, LORD, among the peoples;
I will sing praises to you among the nations.
4 For your faithful love is higher than the heavens,
and your faithfulness reaches to the clouds.
5 God, be exalted above the heavens,
and let your glory be over the whole earth.
6 Save with your right hand and answer me
so that those you love may be rescued.

7 God has spoken in his sanctuary:
"I will celebrate!
I will divide up Shechem.
I will apportion the Valley of Succoth.
8 Gilead is mine, Manasseh is mine,
and Ephraim is my helmet;
Judah is my scepter.
9 Moab is my washbasin;
I throw my sandal on Edom.
I shout in triumph over Philistia."

10 Who will bring me to the fortified city?
Who will lead me to Edom?
11 God, haven't you rejected us?
God, you do not march out with our armies.
12 Give us aid against the foe,
for human help is worthless.
13 With God we will perform valiantly;
he will trample our foes.

Psalm 109

Prayer Against an Enemy

FOR THE CHOIR DIRECTOR. A PSALM OF DAVID.

1 God of my praise, do not be silent.
2 For wicked and deceitful mouths open against me;
they speak against me with lying tongues.
3 They surround me with hateful words
and attack me without cause.
4 In return for my love they accuse me,
but I continue to pray.
5 They repay me evil for good,
and hatred for my love.

6 Set a wicked person over him;
let an accuser stand at his right hand.
7 When he is judged, let him be found guilty,
and let his prayer be counted as sin.
8 Let his days be few;
let another take over his position.
9 Let his children be fatherless
and his wife a widow.
10 Let his children wander as beggars,
searching for food far from their demolished homes.
11 Let a creditor seize all he has;
let strangers plunder what he has worked for.
12 Let no one show him kindness,
and let no one be gracious to his fatherless children.
13 Let the line of his descendants be cut off;
let their name be blotted out in the next generation.
14 Let the iniquity of his fathers
be remembered before the LORD,
and do not let his mother's sin be blotted out.
15 Let their sins always remain before the LORD,
and let him remove all memory of them from the earth.

16 For he did not think to show kindness,
but pursued the suffering, needy, and brokenhearted

in order to put them to death.
17 He loved cursing—let it fall on him;
he took no delight in blessing—let it be far from him.
18 He wore cursing like his coat—
let it enter his body like water
and go into his bones like oil.
19 Let it be like a robe he wraps around himself,
like a belt he always wears.
20 Let this be the LORD's payment to my accusers,
to those who speak evil against me.

21 But you, LORD, my Lord,
deal kindly with me for your name's sake;
because your faithful love is good, rescue me.
22 For I am suffering and needy;
my heart is wounded within me.
23 I fade away like a lengthening shadow;
I am shaken off like a locust.
24 My knees are weak from fasting,
and my body is emaciated.
25 I have become an object of ridicule to my accusers;
when they see me, they shake their heads in scorn.

26 Help me, LORD my God;
save me according to your faithful love
27 so they may know that this is your hand
and that you, LORD, have done it.
28 Though they curse, you will bless.
When they rise up, they will be put to shame,
but your servant will rejoice.
29 My accusers will be clothed with disgrace;
they will wear their shame like a cloak.
30 I will fervently thank the LORD with my mouth;
I will praise him in the presence of many.
31 For he stands at the right hand of the needy
to save him from those who would condemn him.

Psalm 110

The Priestly King

A PSALM OF DAVID.

1 This is the declaration of the LORD
to my Lord:
"Sit at my right hand
until I make your enemies your footstool."
2 The LORD will extend your mighty scepter from Zion.
Rule over your surrounding enemies.
3 Your people will volunteer
on your day of battle.
In holy splendor, from the womb of the dawn,
the dew of your youth belongs to you.
4 The LORD has sworn an oath and will not take it back:
"You are a priest forever
according to the pattern of Melchizedek."

5 The Lord is at your right hand;
he will crush kings on the day of his anger.
6 He will judge the nations, heaping up corpses;
he will crush leaders over the entire world.
7 He will drink from the brook by the road;
therefore, he will lift up his head.

Psalm 111

Praise for the Lord's Works

1 Hallelujah!
I will praise the LORD with all my heart
in the assembly of the upright and in the congregation.
2 The LORD's works are great,
studied by all who delight in them.
3 All that he does is splendid and majestic;
his righteousness endures forever.
4 He has caused his wondrous works to be remembered.
The LORD is gracious and compassionate.
5 He has provided food for those who fear him;
he remembers his covenant forever.
6 He has shown his people the power of his works
by giving them the inheritance of the nations.
7 The works of his hands are truth and justice;
all his instructions are trustworthy.
8 They are established forever and ever,
enacted in truth and in uprightness.
9 He has sent redemption to his people.
He has ordained his covenant forever.
His name is holy and awe-inspiring.

10 The fear of the LORD is the beginning of wisdom;
all who follow his instructions have good insight.
His praise endures forever.

Psalm 112

The Traits of the Righteous

1 Hallelujah!
Happy is the person who fears the LORD,
taking great delight in his commands.
2 His descendants will be powerful in the land;
the generation of the upright will be blessed.
3 Wealth and riches are in his house,
and his righteousness endures forever.
4 Light shines in the darkness for the upright.
He is gracious, compassionate, and righteous.
5 Good will come to the one who lends generously
and conducts his business fairly.
6 He will never be shaken.
The righteous one will be remembered forever.
7 He will not fear bad news;
his heart is confident, trusting in the LORD.
8 His heart is assured; he will not fear.
In the end he will look in triumph on his foes.
9 He distributes freely to the poor;
his righteousness endures forever.
His horn will be exalted in honor.

10 The wicked one will see it and be angry;
he will gnash his teeth in despair.
The desire of the wicked leads to ruin.

Daily Response

Date:

WHAT ATTRIBUTES *of* GOD STOOD OUT TO ME?

HOW DO I CONNECT *with* THE HUMAN EXPERIENCES EXPRESSED *in* TODAY'S PSALMS?

Contextual markers

Poetic devices or patterns

Words or phrases for further study

HOW DO TODAY'S PSALMS GUIDE ME *in the* PRACTICES *of* LENT?

WHAT'S A VERSE *that* I WILL MEDITATE *on* TODAY?

Use Psalm 100 to respond in prayer, allowing the words of Scripture to guide your prayer. Talk to the Lord about whatever the psalm brings to mind. Refer back to the example on page 46 if you need to.

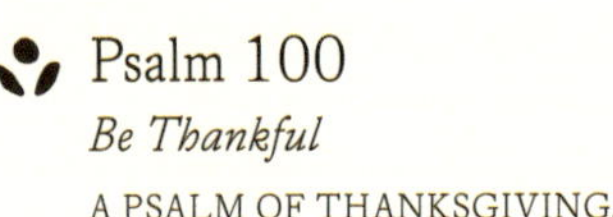

Psalm 100

Be Thankful

A PSALM OF THANKSGIVING.

1 Let the whole earth shout triumphantly to the LORD!

2 Serve the LORD with gladness;
come before him with joyful songs.

3 Acknowledge that the LORD is God.
He made us, and we are his—
his people, the sheep of his pasture.

4 Enter his gates with thanksgiving
and his courts with praise.
Give thanks to him and bless his name.

5 For the LORD is good, and his faithful love
endures forever;
his faithfulness, through all generations.

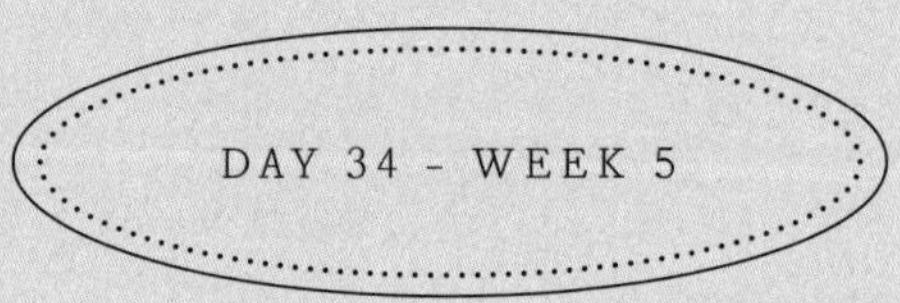

GRACE *Day*

TAKE EACH SATURDAY *to* CATCH UP ON YOUR READING, PRAY, *and* REST *in the* PRESENCE *of the* LORD *with* PASSAGES *from* SCRIPTURE THAT WE TRADITIONALLY READ DURING *the* LENTEN SEASON.

For God was pleased to have
all his fullness dwell in him,
and through him to reconcile
everything to himself,
whether things on earth or things in heaven,
by making peace
through his blood, shed on the cross.

COLOSSIANS 1:19–20

DAY 35 - WEEK 5

WEEKLY TRUTH

SCRIPTURE IS GOD BREATHED *and* TRUE. WHEN WE MEMORIZE IT, WE CARRY HIS WORD *with* US WHEREVER WE GO.

EACH SUNDAY DURING THIS PLAN, WE ARE READING *a* DIFFERENT HALLEL PSALM *and* MEMORIZING ONE *of* ITS VERSES.

THIS WEEK, MEMORIZE PSALM 117:2 AS YOU MEDITATE *on the* PSALM *as a* WHOLE.

Psalm 117

Universal Call to Praise

1 Praise the LORD, all nations!
Glorify him, all peoples!
2 For his faithful love to us is great;
the LORD's faithfulness endures forever.
Hallelujah!

SEE TIPS FOR MEMORIZING SCRIPTURE ON PAGE 272.

MY COMFORT IN MY AFFLICTION

Psalm 119:1–88

THIS IS MY COMFORT *in* MY AFFLICTION: YOUR PROMISE HAS GIVEN ME LIFE.

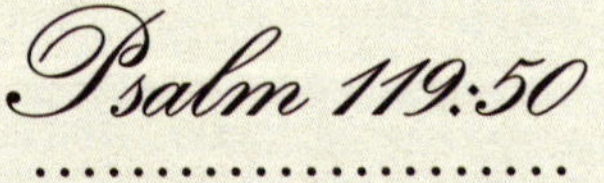

DAY
36

WEEK
6

Psalm 119:1-88

Delight in God's Word

א ALEPH

1 How happy are those whose way is blameless,
who walk according to the LORD's instruction!
2 Happy are those who keep his decrees
and seek him with all their heart.
3 They do nothing wrong;
they walk in his ways.
4 You have commanded that your precepts
be diligently kept.
5 If only my ways were committed
to keeping your statutes!
6 Then I would not be ashamed
when I think about all your commands.
7 I will praise you with an upright heart
when I learn your righteous judgments.
8 I will keep your statutes;
never abandon me.

ב BETH

9 How can a young man keep his way pure?
By keeping your word.
10 I have sought you with all my heart;
don't let me wander from your commands.
11 I have treasured your word in my heart
so that I may not sin against you.
12 LORD, may you be blessed;
teach me your statutes.
13 With my lips I proclaim
all the judgments from your mouth.
14 I rejoice in the way revealed by your decrees
as much as in all riches.
15 I will meditate on your precepts
and think about your ways.
16 I will delight in your statutes;
I will not forget your word.

ג GIMEL

17 Deal generously with your servant
so that I might live;
then I will keep your word.
18 Open my eyes so that I may contemplate
wondrous things from your instruction.

NOTES

19 I am a resident alien on earth;
do not hide your commands from me.
20 I am continually overcome
with longing for your judgments.
21 You rebuke the arrogant,
the ones under a curse,
who wander from your commands.
22 Take insult and contempt away from me,
for I have kept your decrees.
23 Though princes sit together speaking against me,
your servant will think about your statutes;
24 your decrees are my delight
and my counselors.

ד DALETH

25 My life is down in the dust;
give me life through your word.
26 I told you about my life,
and you answered me;
teach me your statutes.
27 Help me understand
the meaning of your precepts
so that I can meditate on your wonders.
28 I am weary from grief;
strengthen me through your word.
29 Keep me from the way of deceit
and graciously give me your instruction.
30 I have chosen the way of truth;
I have set your ordinances before me.
31 I cling to your decrees;
Lord, do not put me to shame.
32 I pursue the way of your commands,
for you broaden my understanding.

ה HE

33 Teach me, Lord, the meaning of your statutes,
and I will always keep them.
34 Help me understand your instruction,
and I will obey it
and follow it with all my heart.
35 Help me stay on the path of your commands,
for I take pleasure in it.
36 Turn my heart to your decrees
and not to dishonest profit.
37 Turn my eyes
from looking at what is worthless;
give me life in your ways.
38 Confirm what you said to your servant,
for it produces reverence for you.
39 Turn away the disgrace I dread;
indeed, your judgments are good.
40 How I long for your precepts!
Give me life through your righteousness.

ו WAW

41 LET YOUR FAITHFUL LOVE
COME TO ME, LORD,
YOUR SALVATION, AS
YOU PROMISED.

42 Then I can answer the one who taunts me,
for I trust in your word.
43 Never take the word of truth from my mouth,
for I hope in your judgments.
44 I will always obey your instruction,
forever and ever.
45 I will walk freely in an open place
because I study your precepts.
46 I will speak of your decrees before kings
and not be ashamed.
47 I delight in your commands,
which I love.
48 I will lift up my hands to your commands,
which I love,
and will meditate on your statutes.

ז ZAYIN

49 Remember your word to your servant;
you have given me hope through it.
50 This is my comfort in my affliction:
Your promise has given me life.
51 The arrogant constantly ridicule me,
but I do not turn away from your instruction.
52 Lord, I remember your judgments from long ago
and find comfort.
53 Fury seizes me because of the wicked
who reject your instruction.

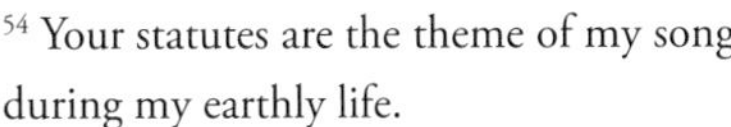

54 Your statutes are the theme of my song
during my earthly life.
55 Lord, I remember your name in the night,
and I obey your instruction.
56 This is my practice:
I obey your precepts.

ח CHETH

57 The Lord is my portion;
I have promised to keep your words.
58 I have sought your favor with all my heart;
be gracious to me according to your promise.
59 I thought about my ways
and turned my steps back to your decrees.
60 I hurried, not hesitating
to keep your commands.
61 Though the ropes of the wicked
were wrapped around me,
I did not forget your instruction.
62 I rise at midnight to thank you
for your righteous judgments.
63 I am a friend to all who fear you,
to those who keep your precepts.
64 Lord, the earth is filled with your faithful love;
teach me your statutes.

ט TETH

65 Lord, you have treated your servant well,
just as you promised.
66 Teach me good judgment and discernment,
for I rely on your commands.
67 Before I was afflicted I went astray,
but now I keep your word.
68 You are good, and you do what is good;
teach me your statutes.
69 The arrogant have smeared me with lies,
but I obey your precepts with all my heart.
70 Their hearts are hard and insensitive,
but I delight in your instruction.
71 It was good for me to be afflicted
so that I could learn your statutes.
72 Instruction from your lips is better for me
than thousands of gold and silver pieces.

י YOD

73 Your hands made me and formed me;
give me understanding
so that I can learn your commands.
74 Those who fear you will see me and rejoice,
for I put my hope in your word.
75 I know, LORD, that your judgments are just
and that you have afflicted me fairly.
76 May your faithful love comfort me
as you promised your servant.
77 May your compassion come to me
so that I may live,
for your instruction is my delight.
78 Let the arrogant be put to shame
for slandering me with lies;
I will meditate on your precepts.
79 Let those who fear you,
those who know your decrees, turn to me.
80 May my heart be blameless regarding your statutes
so that I will not be put to shame.

כ KAPH

81 I long for your salvation;
I put my hope in your word.
82 My eyes grow weary
looking for what you have promised;
I ask, "When will you comfort me?"
83 Though I have become like a wineskin dried by smoke,
I do not forget your statutes.
84 How many days must your servant wait?
When will you execute judgment on my persecutors?
85 The arrogant have dug pits for me;
they violate your instruction.
86 All your commands are true;
people persecute me with lies—help me!
87 They almost ended my life on earth,
but I did not abandon your precepts.
88 Give me life in accordance with your faithful love,
and I will obey the decree you have spoken.

Daily Response

Date:

WHAT ATTRIBUTES *of* GOD STOOD OUT TO ME?

HOW DO I CONNECT *with* THE HUMAN EXPERIENCES EXPRESSED *in* TODAY'S PSALMS?

Contextual markers

Poetic devices or patterns

Words or phrases for further study

HOW DO TODAY'S PSALMS GUIDE ME *in the* PRACTICES *of* LENT?

WHAT'S A VERSE *that* I WILL MEDITATE *on* TODAY?

DAY 37

Psalm 119:89–176

I LONG *for* YOUR SALVATION, LORD

Psalm 119:89–176

ל LAMED

89 LORD, your word is forever;
it is firmly fixed in heaven.
90 Your faithfulness is for all generations;
you established the earth, and it stands firm.
91 Your judgments stand firm today,
for all things are your servants.
92 If your instruction had not been my delight,
I would have died in my affliction.
93 I will never forget your precepts,
for you have given me life through them.
94 I am yours; save me,
for I have studied your precepts.
95 The wicked hope to destroy me,
but I contemplate your decrees.
96 I have seen a limit to all perfection,
but your command is without limit.

מ MEM

97 How I love your instruction!
It is my meditation all day long.
98 Your command makes me wiser than my enemies,
for it is always with me.
99 I have more insight than all my teachers
because your decrees are my meditation.
100 I understand more than the elders
because I obey your precepts.
101 I have kept my feet from every evil path
to follow your word.
102 I have not turned from your judgments,
for you yourself have instructed me.
103 How sweet your word is to my taste—
sweeter than honey in my mouth.
104 I gain understanding from your precepts;
therefore I hate every false way.

נ NUN

105 Your word is a lamp for my feet
and a light on my path.
106 I have solemnly sworn
to keep your righteous judgments.
107 I am severely afflicted;
LORD, give me life according to your word.

108 LORD, please accept my freewill offerings of praise,
and teach me your judgments.
109 My life is constantly in danger,
yet I do not forget your instruction.
110 The wicked have set a trap for me,
but I have not wandered from your precepts.
111 I have your decrees as a heritage forever;
indeed, they are the joy of my heart.
112 I am resolved to obey your statutes
to the very end.

ס SAMEK

113 I hate those who are double-minded,
but I love your instruction.
114 You are my shelter and my shield;
I put my hope in your word.
115 Depart from me, you evil ones,
so that I may obey my God's commands.
116 Sustain me as you promised, and I will live;
do not let me be ashamed of my hope.
117 Sustain me so that I can be safe
and always be concerned about your statutes.
118 You reject all who stray from your statutes,
for their deceit is a lie.
119 You remove all the wicked on earth
as if they were dross from metal;
therefore, I love your decrees.
120 I tremble in awe of you;
I fear your judgments.

ע AYIN

121 I have done what is just and right;
do not leave me to my oppressors.
122 Guarantee your servant's well-being;
do not let the arrogant oppress me.
123 My eyes grow weary looking for your salvation
and for your righteous promise.
124 Deal with your servant based on your faithful love;
teach me your statutes.
125 I am your servant; give me understanding
so that I may know your decrees.
126 It is time for the LORD to act,
for they have violated your instruction.
127 Since I love your commands
more than gold, even the purest gold,
128 I carefully follow all your precepts
and hate every false way.

פ PE

129 Your decrees are wondrous;
therefore I obey them.
130 The revelation of your words brings light
and gives understanding to the inexperienced.
131 I open my mouth and pant
because I long for your commands.
132 Turn to me and be gracious to me,
as is your practice toward those who love your name.
133 Make my steps steady through your promise;
don't let any sin dominate me.
134 Redeem me from human oppression,
and I will keep your precepts.
135 Make your face shine on your servant,
and teach me your statutes.
136 My eyes pour out streams of tears
because people do not follow your instruction.

צ TSADE

137 You are righteous, LORD,
and your judgments are just.
138 The decrees you issue are righteous
and altogether trustworthy.
139 My anger overwhelms me
because my foes forget your words.
140 Your word is completely pure,
and your servant loves it.
141 I am insignificant and despised,
but I do not forget your precepts.
142 Your righteousness is an everlasting righteousness,
and your instruction is true.
143 Trouble and distress have overtaken me,
but your commands are my delight.
144 Your decrees are righteous forever.
Give me understanding, and I will live.

ק QOPH

145 I call with all my heart; answer me, LORD.
I will obey your statutes.
146 I call to you; save me,
and I will keep your decrees.
147 I rise before dawn and cry out for help;

I put my hope in your word.
148 I am awake through each watch of the night
to meditate on your promise.
149 In keeping with your faithful love, hear my voice.
LORD, give me life in keeping with your justice.
150 Those who pursue evil plans come near;
they are far from your instruction.

151 YOU ARE NEAR, LORD,
AND ALL YOUR COMMANDS
ARE TRUE.

152 Long ago I learned from your decrees
that you have established them forever.

ר RESH

153 Consider my affliction and rescue me,
for I have not forgotten your instruction.
154 Champion my cause and redeem me;
give me life as you promised.
155 Salvation is far from the wicked
because they do not study your statutes.
156 Your compassions are many, LORD;
give me life according to your judgments.
157 My persecutors and foes are many.
I have not turned from your decrees.
158 I have seen the disloyal and feel disgust
because they do not keep your word.
159 Consider how I love your precepts;
LORD, give me life according to your faithful love.
160 The entirety of your word is truth,
each of your righteous judgments endures forever.

שׂ SIN

161 Princes have persecuted me without cause,
but my heart fears only your word.
162 I rejoice over your promise
like one who finds vast treasure.
163 I hate and abhor falsehood,
but I love your instruction.
164 I praise you seven times a day
for your righteous judgments.
165 Abundant peace belongs to those
who love your instruction;
nothing makes them stumble.

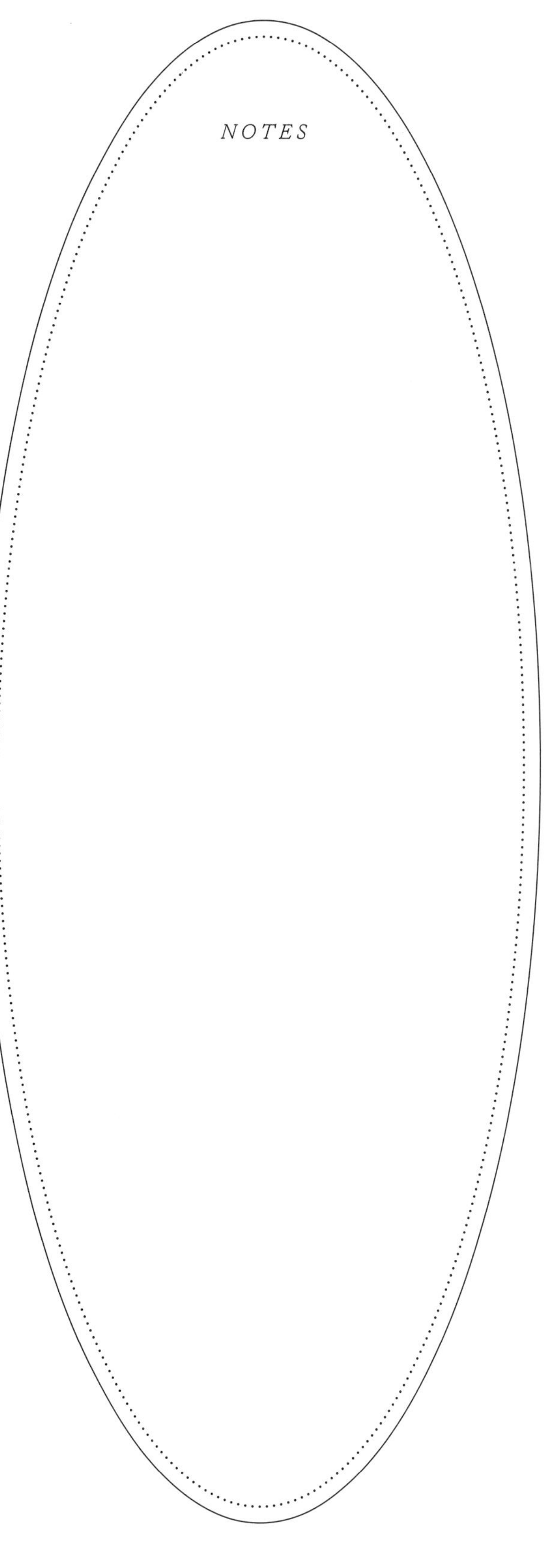

[166] Lord, I hope for your salvation
and carry out your commands.
[167] I obey your decrees
and love them greatly.
[168] I obey your precepts and decrees,
for all my ways are before you.

ת TAW

[169] Let my cry reach you, Lord;
give me understanding according to your word.
[170] Let my plea reach you;
rescue me according to your promise.
[171] My lips pour out praise,
for you teach me your statutes.
[172] My tongue sings about your promise,
for all your commands are righteous.
[173] May your hand be ready to help me,
for I have chosen your precepts.
[174] I long for your salvation, Lord,
and your instruction is my delight.
[175] Let me live, and I will praise you;
may your judgments help me.
[176] I wander like a lost sheep;
seek your servant,
for I do not forget your commands.

Daily Response

Date:

WHAT ATTRIBUTES *of* GOD STOOD OUT TO ME?

HOW DO I CONNECT *with* THE HUMAN EXPERIENCES EXPRESSED *in* TODAY'S PSALMS?

Contextual markers

Poetic devices or patterns

Words or phrases for further study

HOW DO TODAY'S PSALMS GUIDE ME *in the* PRACTICES *of* LENT?

WHAT'S A VERSE *that* I WILL MEDITATE *on* TODAY?

MY HELP COMES FROM *the* LORD

Psalms 120–127

DAY 38  WEEK 6

Psalm 120

A Cry for Truth and Peace

A SONG OF ASCENTS.

1 In my distress I called to the LORD,
and he answered me.
2 "LORD, rescue me from lying lips
and a deceitful tongue."

3 What will he give you,
and what will he do to you,
you deceitful tongue?
4 A warrior's sharp arrows
with burning charcoal!

5 What misery that I have stayed in Meshech,
that I have lived among the tents of Kedar!
6 I have dwelt too long
with those who hate peace.
7 I am for peace; but when I speak,
they are for war.

Psalm 121

The Lord Our Protector

A SONG OF ASCENTS.

1 I lift my eyes toward the mountains.
Where will my help come from?
2 My help comes from the LORD,
the Maker of heaven and earth.

3 He will not allow your foot to slip;
your Protector will not slumber.
4 Indeed, the Protector of Israel
does not slumber or sleep.

5 The LORD protects you;
the LORD is a shelter right by your side.
6 The sun will not strike you by day
or the moon by night.

7 The LORD will protect you from all harm;
he will protect your life.
8 The LORD will protect your coming and going
both now and forever.

Psalm 122

A Prayer for Jerusalem

A SONG OF ASCENTS. OF DAVID.

1 I rejoiced with those who said to me,
"Let's go to the house of the LORD."
2 Our feet were standing
within your gates, Jerusalem—

3 Jerusalem, built as a city should be,
solidly united,
4 where the tribes, the LORD's tribes, go up
to give thanks to the name of the LORD.
(This is an ordinance for Israel.)
5 There, thrones for judgment are placed,
thrones of the house of David.

6 Pray for the well-being of Jerusalem:
"May those who love you be secure;
7 may there be peace within your walls,
security within your fortresses."
8 Because of my brothers and friends,
I will say, "May peace be in you."
9 Because of the house of the LORD our God,
I will pursue your prosperity.

Psalm 123

Looking for God's Favor

A SONG OF ASCENTS.

1 I lift my eyes to you,
the one enthroned in heaven.
2 Like a servant's eyes on his master's hand,
like a servant girl's eyes on her mistress's hand,
so our eyes are on the LORD our God
until he shows us favor.

3 Show us favor, LORD, show us favor,
for we've had more than enough contempt.
4 We've had more than enough
scorn from the arrogant
and contempt from the proud.

Psalm 124

The Lord Is on Our Side

A SONG OF ASCENTS. OF DAVID.

1 If the LORD had not been on our side—
let Israel say—
2 if the LORD had not been on our side
when people attacked us,
3 then they would have swallowed us alive
in their burning anger against us.
4 Then the water would have engulfed us;
the torrent would have swept over us;
5 the raging water would have swept over us.

6 Blessed be the LORD,
who has not let us be ripped apart by their teeth.
7 We have escaped like a bird from the hunter's net;
the net is torn, and we have escaped.
8 Our help is in the name of the LORD,
the Maker of heaven and earth.

Psalm 125

Israel's Stability

A SONG OF ASCENTS.

1 THOSE WHO TRUST IN THE LORD
ARE LIKE MOUNT ZION.
IT CANNOT BE SHAKEN; IT
REMAINS FOREVER.

2 The mountains surround Jerusalem
and the LORD surrounds his people,
both now and forever.

3 The scepter of the wicked will not remain
over the land allotted to the righteous,
so that the righteous will not apply their hands to injustice.
4 Do what is good, LORD, to the good,
to those whose hearts are upright.
5 But as for those who turn aside to crooked ways,
the LORD will banish them with the evildoers.
Peace be with Israel.

Psalm 126

Zion's Restoration

A SONG OF ASCENTS.

1 When the LORD restored the fortunes of Zion,
we were like those who dream.
2 Our mouths were filled with laughter then,
and our tongues with shouts of joy.
Then they said among the nations,
"The LORD has done great things for them."
3 The LORD had done great things for us;
we were joyful.

4 Restore our fortunes, LORD,
like watercourses in the Negev.
5 Those who sow in tears
will reap with shouts of joy.
6 Though one goes along weeping,
carrying the bag of seed,
he will surely come back with shouts of joy,
carrying his sheaves.

Psalm 127

The Blessing of the Lord

A SONG OF ASCENTS. OF SOLOMON.

1 Unless the LORD builds a house,
its builders labor over it in vain;
unless the LORD watches over a city,
the watchman stays alert in vain.
2 In vain you get up early and stay up late,
working hard to have enough food—
yes, he gives sleep to the one he loves.

3 Sons are indeed a heritage from the LORD,
offspring, a reward.
4 Like arrows in the hand of a warrior
are the sons born in one's youth.
5 Happy is the man who has filled his quiver with them.
They will never be put to shame
when they speak with their enemies at the city gate.

Daily Response

Date:

WHAT ATTRIBUTES *of* GOD STOOD OUT TO ME?

HOW DO I CONNECT *with* THE HUMAN EXPERIENCES EXPRESSED *in* TODAY'S PSALMS?

Contextual markers

Poetic devices or patterns

Words or phrases for further study

HOW DO TODAY'S PSALMS GUIDE ME *in the* PRACTICES *of* LENT?

WHAT'S A VERSE *that* I WILL MEDITATE *on* TODAY?

Redemption in Abundance

PSALMS 128–134

DAY 39 ………………… WEEK 6

Psalm 128

Blessings for Those Who Fear God

A SONG OF ASCENTS.

1 How happy is everyone who fears the LORD,
who walks in his ways!
2 You will surely eat
what your hands have worked for.
You will be happy,
and it will go well for you.
3 Your wife will be like a fruitful vine
within your house,
your children, like young olive trees
around your table.
4 In this very way
the man who fears the LORD
will be blessed.

5 May the LORD bless you from Zion,
so that you will see the prosperity of Jerusalem
all the days of your life
6 and will see your children's children!
Peace be with Israel.

Psalm 129

Protection of the Oppressed

A SONG OF ASCENTS.

1 Since my youth they have often attacked me—
let Israel say—
2 since my youth they have often attacked me,
but they have not prevailed against me.
3 Plowmen plowed over my back;
they made their furrows long.
4 The LORD is righteous;
he has cut the ropes of the wicked.

5 Let all who hate Zion
be driven back in disgrace.
6 Let them be like grass on the rooftops,
which withers before it grows up
7 and can't even fill the hands of the reaper
or the arms of the one who binds sheaves.
8 Then none who pass by will say,
"May the LORD's blessing be on you.
We bless you in the name of the LORD."

Psalm 130

Awaiting Redemption

A SONG OF ASCENTS.

1 Out of the depths I call to you, LORD!
2 Lord, listen to my voice;
let your ears be attentive
to my cry for help.

[3] Lord, if you kept an account of iniquities,
Lord, who could stand?
[4] But with you there is forgiveness,
so that you may be revered.

[5] I wait for the Lord; I wait
and put my hope in his word.
[6] I wait for the Lord
more than watchmen for the morning—
more than watchmen for the morning.

[7] Israel, put your hope in the Lord.
For there is faithful love with the Lord,
and with him is redemption in abundance.
[8] And he will redeem Israel
from all its iniquities.

Psalm 131

A Childlike Spirit

A SONG OF ASCENTS. OF DAVID.

[1] Lord, my heart is not proud;
my eyes are not haughty.
I do not get involved with things
too great or too wondrous for me.
[2] Instead, I have calmed and quieted my soul
like a weaned child with its mother;
my soul is like a weaned child.

[3] Israel, put your hope in the Lord,
both now and forever.

Psalm 132

David and Zion Chosen

A SONG OF ASCENTS.

[1] Lord, remember David
and all the hardships he endured,
[2] and how he swore an oath to the Lord,
making a vow to the Mighty One of Jacob:
[3] "I will not enter my house
or get into my bed,
[4] I will not allow my eyes to sleep
or my eyelids to slumber

5 until I find a place for the Lord,
a dwelling for the Mighty One of Jacob."

6 We heard of the ark in Ephrathah;
we found it in the fields of Jaar.
7 Let's go to his dwelling place;
let's worship at his footstool.
8 Rise up, Lord, come to your resting place,
you and your powerful ark.
9 May your priests be clothed with righteousness,
and may your faithful people shout for joy.
10 For the sake of your servant David,
do not reject your anointed one.

11 The Lord swore an oath to David,
a promise he will not abandon:
"I will set one of your offspring
on your throne.
12 If your sons keep my covenant
and my decrees that I will teach them,
their sons will also sit on your throne forever."

13 For the Lord has chosen Zion;
he has desired it for his home:
14 "This is my resting place forever;
I will make my home here
because I have desired it.
15 I will abundantly bless its food;
I will satisfy its needy with bread.
16 I will clothe its priests with salvation,
and its faithful people will shout for joy.
17 There I will make a horn grow for David;
I have prepared a lamp for my anointed one.
18 I will clothe his enemies with shame,
but the crown he wears will be glorious."

Psalm 133

Living in Harmony

A SONG OF ASCENTS. OF DAVID.

1 How delightfully good
when brothers live together in harmony!
2 It is like fine oil on the head,
running down on the beard,
running down Aaron's beard
onto his robes.
3 It is like the dew of Hermon
falling on the mountains of Zion.
For there the Lord has appointed the blessing—
life forevermore.

Psalm 134

Call to Evening Worship

A SONG OF ASCENTS.

1 Now bless the Lord,
all you servants of the Lord
who stand in the Lord's house at night!
2 Lift up your hands in the holy place
and bless the Lord!

3 May the Lord,
Maker of heaven and earth,
bless you from Zion.

Daily Response

Date:

WHAT ATTRIBUTES *of* GOD STOOD OUT TO ME?

HOW DO I CONNECT *with* THE HUMAN EXPERIENCES EXPRESSED *in* TODAY'S PSALMS?

Contextual markers

Poetic devices or patterns

Words or phrases for further study

HOW DO TODAY'S PSALMS GUIDE ME *in the* PRACTICES *of* LENT?

WHAT'S A VERSE *that* I WILL MEDITATE *on* TODAY?

DAY 40

PSALMS 135–139

WEEK 6

YOUR WORKS ARE WONDERFUL

Psalm 135

The Lord Is Great

1 Hallelujah!
Praise the name of the Lord.
Give praise, you servants of the Lord
2 who stand in the house of the Lord,
in the courts of the house of our God.
3 Praise the Lord, for the Lord is good;
sing praise to his name, for it is delightful.
4 For the Lord has chosen Jacob for himself,
Israel as his treasured possession.

5 For I know that the Lord is great;
our Lord is greater than all gods.
6 The Lord does whatever he pleases
in heaven and on earth,
in the seas and all the depths.
7 He causes the clouds to rise from the ends of the earth.
He makes lightning for the rain
and brings the wind from his storehouses.

8 He struck down the firstborn of Egypt,
both people and animals.
9 He sent signs and wonders against you, Egypt,
against Pharaoh and all his officials.
10 He struck down many nations
and slaughtered mighty kings:
11 Sihon king of the Amorites,
Og king of Bashan,
and all the kings of Canaan.
12 He gave their land as an inheritance,
an inheritance to his people Israel.

13 Lord, your name endures forever,
your reputation, Lord,
through all generations.
14 For the Lord will vindicate his people
and have compassion on his servants.

15 The idols of the nations are of silver and gold,
made by human hands.
16 They have mouths but cannot speak,
eyes, but cannot see.
17 They have ears but cannot hear;
indeed, there is no breath in their mouths.
18 Those who make them are just like them,
as are all who trust in them.

19 House of Israel, bless the Lord!
House of Aaron, bless the Lord!
20 House of Levi, bless the Lord!
You who revere the Lord, bless the Lord!
21 Blessed be the Lord from Zion;
he dwells in Jerusalem.
Hallelujah!

Psalm 136

God's Love Is Eternal

1 Give thanks to the Lord, for he is good.
His faithful love endures forever.
2 Give thanks to the God of gods.

His faithful love endures forever.
3 Give thanks to the Lord of lords.
His faithful love endures forever.
4 He alone does great wonders.
His faithful love endures forever.
5 He made the heavens skillfully.
His faithful love endures forever.
6 He spread the land on the waters.
His faithful love endures forever.
7 He made the great lights:
His faithful love endures forever.
8 the sun to rule by day,
His faithful love endures forever.
9 the moon and stars to rule by night.
His faithful love endures forever.
10 He struck the firstborn of the Egyptians
His faithful love endures forever.
11 and brought Israel out from among them
His faithful love endures forever.
12 with a strong hand and outstretched arm.
His faithful love endures forever.
13 He divided the Red Sea
His faithful love endures forever.
14 and led Israel through,
His faithful love endures forever.
15 but hurled Pharaoh and his army into the Red Sea.
His faithful love endures forever.
16 He led his people in the wilderness.
His faithful love endures forever.
17 He struck down great kings
His faithful love endures forever.
18 and slaughtered famous kings—
His faithful love endures forever.
19 Sihon king of the Amorites
His faithful love endures forever.
20 and Og king of Bashan—
His faithful love endures forever.
21 and gave their land as an inheritance,
His faithful love endures forever.
22 an inheritance to Israel his servant.
His faithful love endures forever.
23 He remembered us in our humiliation
His faithful love endures forever.
24 and rescued us from our foes.
His faithful love endures forever.
25 He gives food to every creature.
His faithful love endures forever.
26 Give thanks to the God of heaven!
His faithful love endures forever.

Psalm 137

Lament of the Exiles

1 By the rivers of Babylon—
there we sat down and wept
when we remembered Zion.
2 There we hung up our lyres
on the poplar trees,
3 for our captors there asked us for songs,
and our tormentors, for rejoicing:
"Sing us one of the songs of Zion."

4 How can we sing the Lord's song
on foreign soil?
5 If I forget you, Jerusalem,
may my right hand forget its skill.
6 May my tongue stick to the roof of my mouth
if I do not remember you,
if I do not exalt Jerusalem as my greatest joy!

7 Remember, Lord, what the Edomites said
that day at Jerusalem:
"Destroy it! Destroy it
down to its foundations!"
8 Daughter Babylon, doomed to destruction,
happy is the one who pays you back
what you have done to us.
9 Happy is he who takes your little ones
and dashes them against the rocks.

Psalm 138

A Thankful Heart

OF DAVID.

1 I will give you thanks with all my heart;
I will sing your praise before the heavenly beings.
2 I will bow down toward your holy temple
and give thanks to your name
for your constant love and truth.

You have exalted your name
and your promise above everything else.
3 On the day I called, you answered me;
you increased strength within me.

4 All the kings on earth will give you thanks, LORD,
when they hear what you have promised.
5 They will sing of the LORD's ways,
for the LORD's glory is great.
6 Though the LORD is exalted,
he takes note of the humble;
but he knows the haughty from a distance.

7 If I walk into the thick of danger,
you will preserve my life
from the anger of my enemies.
You will extend your hand;
your right hand will save me.
8 The LORD will fulfill his purpose for me.
LORD, your faithful love endures forever;
do not abandon the work of your hands.

Psalm 139

The All-Knowing, Ever-Present God

FOR THE CHOIR DIRECTOR. A PSALM OF DAVID.

1 LORD, you have searched me and known me.
2 You know when I sit down and when I stand up;
you understand my thoughts from far away.
3 You observe my travels and my rest;
you are aware of all my ways.
4 Before a word is on my tongue,
you know all about it, LORD.

5 YOU HAVE ENCIRCLED ME;
YOU HAVE PLACED YOUR HAND
ON ME.

6 This wondrous knowledge is beyond me.
It is lofty; I am unable to reach it.

7 Where can I go to escape your Spirit?
Where can I flee from your presence?
8 If I go up to heaven, you are there;

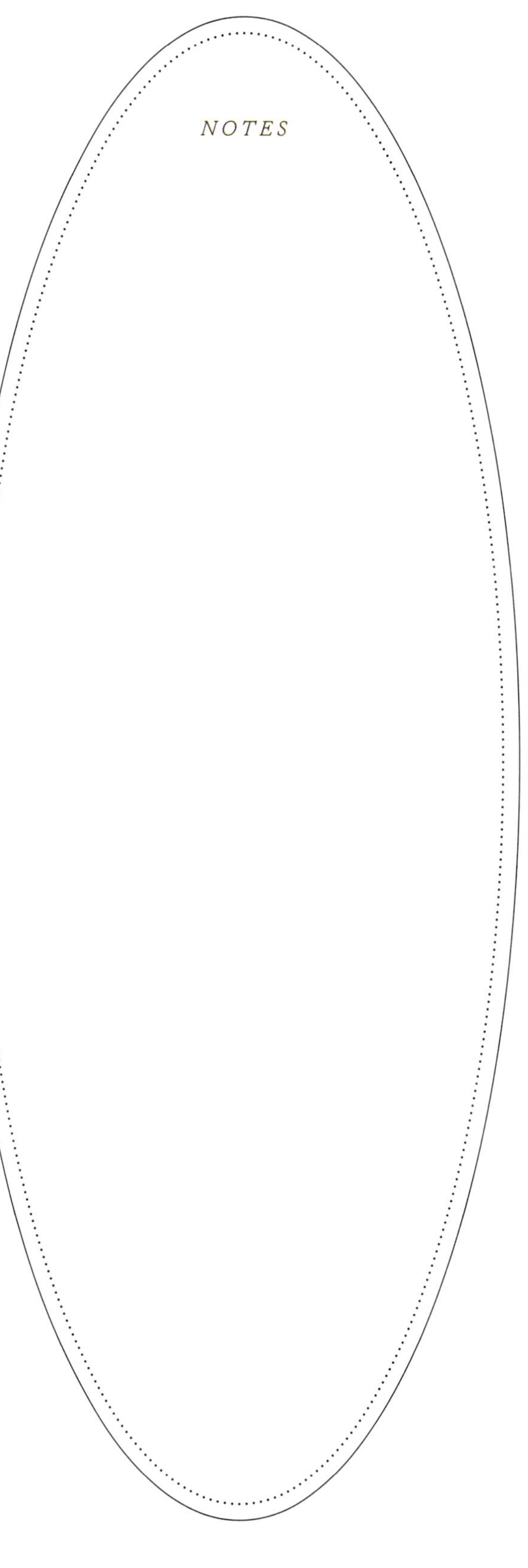

if I make my bed in Sheol, you are there.
9 If I fly on the wings of the dawn
and settle down on the western horizon,
10 even there your hand will lead me;
your right hand will hold on to me.
11 If I say, "Surely the darkness will hide me,
and the light around me will be night"—
12 even the darkness is not dark to you.
The night shines like the day;
darkness and light are alike to you.

13 For it was you who created my inward parts;
you knit me together in my mother's womb.
14 I will praise you
because I have been remarkably and wondrously made.
Your works are wondrous,
and I know this very well.
15 My bones were not hidden from you
when I was made in secret,
when I was formed in the depths of the earth.
16 Your eyes saw me when I was formless;
all my days were written in your book and planned
before a single one of them began.

17 God, how precious your thoughts are to me;
how vast their sum is!
18 If I counted them,
they would outnumber the grains of sand;
when I wake up, I am still with you.

19 God, if only you would kill the wicked—
you bloodthirsty men, stay away from me—
20 who invoke you deceitfully.
Your enemies swear by you falsely.
21 LORD, don't I hate those who hate you,
and detest those who rebel against you?
22 I hate them with extreme hatred;
I consider them my enemies.

23 Search me, God, and know my heart;
test me and know my concerns.
24 See if there is any offensive way in me;
lead me in the everlasting way.

Daily Response

Date:

WHAT ATTRIBUTES *of* GOD STOOD OUT TO ME?

HOW DO I CONNECT *with* THE HUMAN EXPERIENCES EXPRESSED *in* TODAY'S PSALMS?

Contextual markers

Poetic devices or patterns

Words or phrases for further study

HOW DO TODAY'S PSALMS GUIDE ME *in the* PRACTICES *of* LENT?

WHAT'S A VERSE *that* I WILL MEDITATE *on* TODAY?

Use Psalm 130 to respond in prayer, allowing the words of Scripture to guide your prayer. Talk to the Lord about whatever the psalm brings to mind. Refer back to the example on page 46 if you need to.

Psalm 130

Awaiting Redemption

A SONG OF ASCENTS.

1 Out of the depths I call to you, LORD!

2 LORD, listen to my voice;
let your ears be attentive
to my cry for help.

3 LORD, if you kept an account of iniquities,
Lord, who could stand?

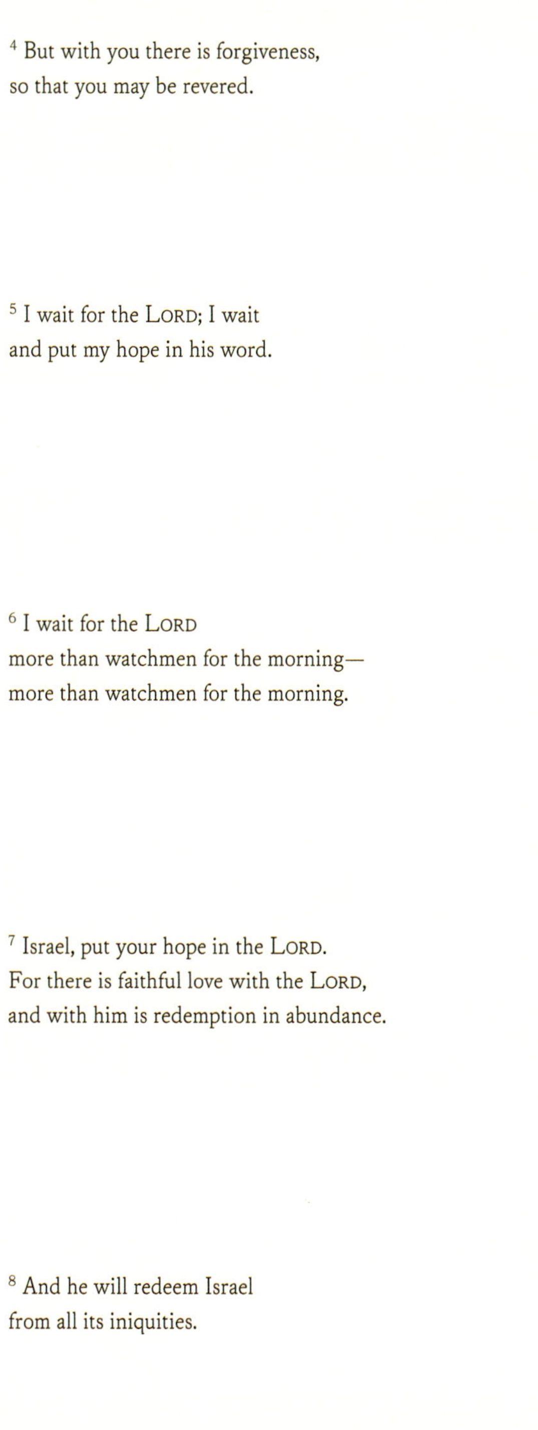

[4] But with you there is forgiveness,
so that you may be revered.

[5] I wait for the LORD; I wait
and put my hope in his word.

[6] I wait for the LORD
more than watchmen for the morning—
more than watchmen for the morning.

[7] Israel, put your hope in the LORD.
For there is faithful love with the LORD,
and with him is redemption in abundance.

[8] And he will redeem Israel
from all its iniquities.

GRACE *Day*

TAKE EACH SATURDAY *to* CATCH UP ON YOUR READING, PRAY, *and* REST *in the* PRESENCE *of the* LORD *with* PASSAGES *from* SCRIPTURE THAT WE TRADITIONALLY READ DURING *the* LENTEN SEASON.

But he was pierced because of our rebellion,
crushed because of our iniquities;
punishment for our peace was on him,
and we are healed by his wounds.
We all went astray like sheep;
we all have turned to our own way;
and the LORD has punished him
for the iniquity of us all.

ISAIAH 53:5–6

DAY 42 - WEEK 6

WEEKLY TRUTH

SCRIPTURE IS GOD BREATHED *and* TRUE. WHEN WE MEMORIZE IT, WE CARRY HIS WORD *with* US WHEREVER WE GO.

EACH SUNDAY DURING THIS PLAN, WE ARE READING *a* DIFFERENT HALLEL PSALM *and* MEMORIZING ONE *of* ITS VERSES.

THIS WEEK, MEMORIZE PSALM 118:14 AS YOU MEDITATE *on the* PSALM *as a* WHOLE.

Psalm 118

Thanksgiving for Victory

1 Give thanks to the LORD, for he is good;
his faithful love endures forever.
2 Let Israel say,
"His faithful love endures forever."
3 Let the house of Aaron say,
"His faithful love endures forever."
4 Let those who fear the LORD say,
"His faithful love endures forever."

5 I called to the LORD in distress;
the LORD answered me
and put me in a spacious place.
6 The LORD is for me; I will not be afraid.
What can a mere mortal do to me?
7 The LORD is my helper;
therefore, I will look in triumph on those who hate me.

8 It is better to take refuge in the LORD
than to trust in humanity.
9 It is better to take refuge in the LORD
than to trust in nobles.

10 All the nations surrounded me;
in the name of the LORD I destroyed them.
11 They surrounded me, yes, they surrounded me;
in the name of the LORD I destroyed them.
12 They surrounded me like bees;
they were extinguished like a fire among thorns;
in the name of the LORD I destroyed them.
13 They pushed me hard to make me fall,
but the LORD helped me.
14 The LORD is my strength and my song;
he has become my salvation.

15 There are shouts of joy and victory
in the tents of the righteous:
"The LORD's right hand performs valiantly!
16 The LORD's right hand is raised.
The LORD's right hand performs valiantly!"
17 I will not die, but I will live
and proclaim what the LORD has done.
18 The LORD disciplined me severely
but did not give me over to death.

19 Open the gates of righteousness for me;
I will enter through them
and give thanks to the LORD.
20 This is the LORD's gate;
the righteous will enter through it.
21 I will give thanks to you
because you have answered me
and have become my salvation.
22 The stone that the builders rejected
has become the cornerstone.
23 This came from the LORD;
it is wondrous in our sight.
24 This is the day the LORD has made;
let's rejoice and be glad in it.

25 LORD, save us!
LORD, please grant us success!
26 He who comes in the name
of the LORD is blessed.
From the house of the LORD we bless you.
27 The LORD is God and has given us light.
Bind the festival sacrifice with cords
to the horns of the altar.
28 You are my God, and I will give you thanks.
You are my God; I will exalt you.
29 Give thanks to the LORD, for he is good;
his faithful love endures forever.

SEE TIPS FOR MEMORIZING SCRIPTURE ON PAGE 272.

DAY 43

Psalms 140–143

MY EYES LOOK

to YOU, LORD

Psalm 140

Prayer for Rescue

FOR THE CHOIR DIRECTOR. A PSALM OF DAVID.

1 Rescue me, LORD, from evil men.
Keep me safe from violent men
2 who plan evil in their hearts.
They stir up wars all day long.
3 They make their tongues
as sharp as a snake's bite;
viper's venom is under their lips. *Selah*

4 Protect me, LORD,
from the power of the wicked.
Keep me safe from violent men
who plan to make me stumble.
5 The proud hide a trap with ropes for me;
they spread a net along the path
and set snares for me. *Selah*

6 I say to the LORD, "You are my God."
Listen, LORD, to my cry for help.
7 LORD, my Lord, my strong Savior,
you shield my head on the day of battle.
8 LORD, do not grant the desires of the wicked;
do not let them achieve their goals.
Otherwise, they will become proud. *Selah*

9 When those who surround me rise up,
may the trouble their lips cause overwhelm them.
10 Let hot coals fall on them.
Let them be thrown into the fire,
into the abyss, never again to rise.
11 Do not let a slanderer stay in the land.
Let evil relentlessly hunt down a violent man.

12 I know that the LORD upholds
the just cause of the poor,
justice for the needy.
13 Surely the righteous will praise your name;
the upright will live in your presence.

Psalm 141

Protection from Sin and Sinners

A PSALM OF DAVID.

1 LORD, I call on you; hurry to help me.
Listen to my voice when I call on you.
2 May my prayer be set before you as incense,
the raising of my hands as the evening offering.

3 LORD, set up a guard for my mouth;
keep watch at the door of my lips.
4 Do not let my heart turn to any evil thing
or perform wicked acts with evildoers.
Do not let me feast on their delicacies.
5 Let the righteous one strike me—
it is an act of faithful love;
let him rebuke me—
it is oil for my head;
let me not refuse it.
Even now my prayer is against
the evil acts of the wicked.
6 When their rulers will be thrown off
the sides of a cliff,
the people will listen to my words,
for they are pleasing.

7 As when one plows and breaks up the soil,
turning up rocks,
so our bones have been scattered
at the mouth of Sheol.

8 But my eyes look to you, LORD, my Lord.
I seek refuge in you; do not let me die.
9 Protect me from the trap they have set for me,
and from the snares of evildoers.
10 Let the wicked fall into their own nets,
while I pass by safely.

Psalm 142

A Cry of Distress

A *MASKIL* OF DAVID. WHEN HE WAS IN THE CAVE. A PRAYER.

1 I cry aloud to the LORD;
I plead aloud to the LORD for mercy.
2 I pour out my complaint before him;
I reveal my trouble to him.
3 Although my spirit is weak within me,
you know my way.
Along this path I travel
they have hidden a trap for me.
4 Look to the right and see:
no one stands up for me;
there is no refuge for me;
no one cares about me.

5 I cry to you, LORD;
I say, "You are my shelter,
my portion in the land of the living."
6 Listen to my cry,
for I am very weak.
Rescue me from those who pursue me,
for they are too strong for me.
7 Free me from prison
so that I can praise your name.
The righteous will gather around me
because you deal generously with me.

Psalm 143

A Cry for Help

A PSALM OF DAVID.

1 LORD, hear my prayer.
In your faithfulness listen to my plea,
and in your righteousness answer me.
2 Do not bring your servant into judgment,
for no one alive is righteous in your sight.

3 For the enemy has pursued me,
crushing me to the ground,
making me live in darkness
like those long dead.
4 My spirit is weak within me;
my heart is overcome with dismay.

5 I remember the days of old;
I meditate on all you have done;
I reflect on the work of your hands.
6 I spread out my hands to you;
I am like parched land before you. *Selah*

7 Answer me quickly, LORD;
my spirit fails.
Don't hide your face from me,
or I will be like those
going down to the Pit.
8 Let me experience
your faithful love in the morning,
for I trust in you.
Reveal to me the way I should go
because I appeal to you.
9 Rescue me from my enemies, LORD;
I come to you for protection.
10 Teach me to do your will,
for you are my God.
May your gracious Spirit
lead me on level ground.

11 For your name's sake, LORD,
let me live.
In your righteousness deliver me from trouble,
12 and in your faithful love destroy my enemies.
Wipe out all those who attack me,
for I am your servant.

Daily Response

Date:

WHAT ATTRIBUTES *of* GOD STOOD OUT TO ME?

HOW DO I CONNECT *with* THE HUMAN EXPERIENCES EXPRESSED *in* TODAY'S PSALMS?

Contextual markers

Poetic devices or patterns

Words or phrases for further study

HOW DO TODAY'S PSALMS GUIDE ME *in the* PRACTICES *of* LENT?

WHAT'S A VERSE *that* I WILL MEDITATE *on* TODAY?

WHEN JESUS *Quotes the Psalms*

✿ ✿ ✿

The psalms are some of the Old Testament passages Jesus most frequently quoted. He referenced parts of the book of Psalms in both His teachings and personal interactions with God, affirming His identity and purpose as the Messiah. As you read through these passages from the Gospels, take note of how Jesus Himself used the psalms in His own prayers and speech.

Jesus's Use of the Psalms

		Reference
Mt 7:21–23	"Not everyone who says to me, 'Lord, Lord,' will enter the kingdom of heaven, but only the one who does the will of my Father in heaven. On that day many will say to me, 'Lord, Lord, didn't we prophesy in your name, drive out demons in your name, and do many miracles in your name?' Then I will announce to them, 'I never knew you. Depart from me, you lawbreakers!'"	Ps 6:8
Mt 13:34–35	Jesus told the crowds all these things in parables, and he did not tell them anything without a parable, so that what was spoken through the prophet might be fulfilled: I will open my mouth in parables; I will declare things kept secret from the foundation of the world.	Ps 78:2
Mt 21:14–16	The blind and the lame came to him in the temple, and he healed them. When the chief priests and the scribes saw the wonders that he did and the children shouting in the temple, "*Hosanna* to the Son of David!" they were indignant and said to him, "Do you hear what these children are saying?" Jesus replied, "Yes, have you never read: You have prepared praise from the mouths of infants and nursing babies?"	Ps 8:2
Mt 21:42–44 (also appears in Mk 12:10–12; Lk 20:17–18)	Jesus said to them, "Have you never read in the Scriptures: The stone that the builders rejected has become the cornerstone. This is what the Lord has done and it is wonderful in our eyes? Therefore I tell you, the kingdom of God will be taken away from you and given to a people producing its fruit. Whoever falls on this stone will be broken to pieces; but on whomever it falls, it will shatter him."	Ps 118:22–23

Jesus's Use of the Psalms		Reference
Mt 23:39 (also appears in Lk 13:35)	"For I tell you, you will not see me again until you say, 'Blessed is he who comes in the name of the Lord'!"	Ps 118:26
Mk 12:35–37 (also appears in Mt 22:43–46; Lk 20:42–44)	While Jesus was teaching in the temple, he asked, "How can the scribes say that the Messiah is the son of David? David himself says by the Holy Spirit: The Lord declared to my Lord, 'Sit at my right hand until I put your enemies under your feet.' David himself calls him 'Lord.' How, then, can he be his son?" And the large crowd was listening to him with delight.	Ps 110:1
Mk 14:61–62 (also appears in Mt 26:63–64)	But he kept silent and did not answer. Again the high priest questioned him, "Are you the Messiah, the Son of the Blessed One?" "I am," said Jesus, "and you will see the Son of Man seated at the right hand of Power and coming with the clouds of heaven."	Ps 110:1
Mk 15:34 (also appears in Mt 27:46)	And at three Jesus cried out with a loud voice, *"Eloi, Eloi, lemá sabachthání?"* which is translated, "My God, my God, why have you abandoned me?"	Ps 22:1

Jesus's Use of the Psalms | *Reference*

Lk 23:46	And Jesus called out with a loud voice, "Father, into your hands I entrust my spirit." Saying this, he breathed his last.	Ps 31:5
Jn 10:34–38	Jesus answered them, "Isn't it written in your law, I said, you are gods? If he called those to whom the word of God came 'gods'—and the Scripture cannot be broken—do you say, 'You are blaspheming' to the one the Father set apart and sent into the world, because I said: I am the Son of God? If I am not doing my Father's works, don't believe me. But if I am doing them and you don't believe me, believe the works. This way you will know and understand that the Father is in me and I in the Father."	Ps 82:6
Jn 13:18–19	"I'm not speaking about all of you; I know those I have chosen. But the Scripture must be fulfilled: The one who eats my bread has raised his heel against me. I am telling you now before it happens, so that when it does happen you will believe that I am he."	Ps 41:9
Jn 15:24–25	If I had not done the works among them that no one else has done, they would not be guilty of sin. Now they have seen and hated both me and my Father. But this happened so that the statement written in their law might be fulfilled: They hated me for no reason.	Ps 69:4

PSALMS 144–146

DAY
44

WEEK
7

THE LORD REIGNS FOREVER

Psalm 144

A King's Prayer

OF DAVID.

1 Blessed be the LORD, my rock
who trains my hands for battle
and my fingers for warfare.
2 He is my faithful love and my fortress,
my stronghold and my deliverer.
He is my shield, and I take refuge in him;
he subdues my people under me.

3 LORD, what is a human that you care for him,
a son of man that you think of him?
4 A human is like a breath;
his days are like a passing shadow.

5 LORD, part your heavens and come down.
Touch the mountains, and they will smoke.
6 Flash your lightning and scatter the foe;
shoot your arrows and rout them.
7 Reach down from on high;
rescue me from deep water, and set me free
from the grasp of foreigners
8 whose mouths speak lies,
whose right hands are deceptive.

9 God, I will sing a new song to you;
I will play on a ten-stringed harp for you—
10 the one who gives victory to kings,
who frees his servant David
from the deadly sword.

11 Set me free and rescue me
from foreigners
whose mouths speak lies,
whose right hands are deceptive.

12 Then our sons will be like plants
nurtured in their youth,
our daughters, like corner pillars
that are carved in the palace style.
13 Our storehouses will be full,
supplying all kinds of produce;
our flocks will increase by thousands
and tens of thousands in our open fields.
14 Our cattle will be well fed.
There will be no breach in the walls,
no going into captivity,
and no cry of lament in our public squares.
15 Happy are the people with such blessings.
Happy are the people whose God is the LORD.

Psalm 145

Praising God's Greatness

A HYMN OF DAVID.

1 I exalt you, my God the King,
and bless your name forever and ever.
2 I will bless you every day;
I will praise your name forever and ever.

[3] The Lord is great and is highly praised;
his greatness is unsearchable.
[4] One generation will declare your works to the next
and will proclaim your mighty acts.
[5] I will speak of your splendor and glorious majesty
and your wondrous works.
[6] They will proclaim the power of your
awe-inspiring acts,
and I will declare your greatness.
[7] They will give a testimony of your great goodness
and will joyfully sing of your righteousness.

[8] The Lord is gracious and compassionate,
slow to anger and great in faithful love.
[9] The Lord is good to everyone;
his compassion rests on all he has made.
[10] All you have made will thank you, Lord;
the faithful will bless you.
[11] They will speak of the glory of your kingdom
and will declare your might,
[12] informing all people of your mighty acts
and of the glorious splendor of your kingdom.
[13] Your kingdom is an everlasting kingdom;
your rule is for all generations.
The Lord is faithful in all his words
and gracious in all his actions.

[14] The Lord helps all who fall;
he raises up all who are oppressed.
[15] All eyes look to you,
and you give them their food at the proper time.
[16] You open your hand
and satisfy the desire of every living thing.

[17] The Lord is righteous in all his ways
and faithful in all his acts.
[18] The Lord is near all who call out to him,
all who call out to him with integrity.
[19] He fulfills the desires of those who fear him;
he hears their cry for help and saves them.
[20] The Lord guards all those who love him,
but he destroys all the wicked.
[21] My mouth will declare the Lord's praise;
let every living thing
bless his holy name forever and ever.

Psalm 146

The God of Compassion

[1] Hallelujah!
My soul, praise the Lord.
[2] I will praise the Lord all my life;
I will sing to my God as long as I live.

[3] Do not trust in nobles,
in a son of man, who cannot save.
[4] When his breath leaves him,
he returns to the ground;
on that day his plans die.

[5] Happy is the one whose help is the God of Jacob,
whose hope is in the Lord his God,
[6] the Maker of heaven and earth,
the sea and everything in them.
He remains faithful forever,
[7] executing justice for the exploited
and giving food to the hungry.
The Lord frees prisoners.
[8] The Lord opens the eyes of the blind.
The Lord raises up those who are oppressed.
The Lord loves the righteous.
[9] The Lord protects resident aliens
and helps the fatherless and the widow,
but he frustrates the ways of the wicked.

[10] The Lord reigns forever;
Zion, your God reigns for all generations.
Hallelujah!

Daily Response

Date:

WHAT ATTRIBUTES *of* GOD STOOD OUT TO ME?

HOW DO I CONNECT *with* THE HUMAN EXPERIENCES EXPRESSED *in* TODAY'S PSALMS?

Contextual markers

Poetic devices or patterns

Words or phrases for further study

HOW DO TODAY'S PSALMS GUIDE ME *in the* PRACTICES *of* LENT?

WHAT'S A VERSE *that* I WILL MEDITATE *on* TODAY?

PSALMS 147–150

HOW GOOD IT IS *to* SING *to* OUR GOD

Hallelujah! How good it is to sing to our God, for praise is pleasant and lovely.

Psalm 147:1

Psalm 147

God Restores Jerusalem

1 Hallelujah!
How good it is to sing to our God,
for praise is pleasant and lovely.

2 The LORD rebuilds Jerusalem;
he gathers Israel's exiled people.
3 He heals the brokenhearted
and bandages their wounds.
4 He counts the number of the stars;
he gives names to all of them.
5 Our Lord is great, vast in power;
his understanding is infinite.
6 The LORD helps the oppressed
but brings the wicked to the ground.

7 Sing to the LORD with thanksgiving;
play the lyre to our God,
8 who covers the sky with clouds,
prepares rain for the earth,
and causes grass to grow on the hills.
9 He provides the animals with their food,
and the young ravens what they cry for.

10 He is not impressed by the strength of a horse;
he does not value the power of a warrior.
11 The LORD values those who fear him,
those who put their hope in his faithful love.

12 Exalt the LORD, Jerusalem;
praise your God, Zion!
13 For he strengthens the bars of your city gates
and blesses your children within you.
14 He endows your territory with prosperity;
he satisfies you with the finest wheat.

15 He sends his command throughout the earth;
his word runs swiftly.
16 He spreads snow like wool;
he scatters frost like ashes;
17 he throws his hailstones like crumbs.
Who can withstand his cold?
18 He sends his word and melts them;
he unleashes his winds, and the water flows.
19 He declares his word to Jacob,
his statutes and judgments to Israel.
20 He has not done this for every nation;
they do not know his judgments.
Hallelujah!

Psalm 148

Creation's Praise of the Lord

1 Hallelujah!
Praise the LORD from the heavens;
praise him in the heights.
2 Praise him, all his angels;
praise him, all his heavenly armies.
3 Praise him, sun and moon;
praise him, all you shining stars.
4 Praise him, highest heavens,
and you waters above the heavens.
5 Let them praise the name of the LORD,
for he commanded, and they were created.
6 He set them in position forever and ever;
he gave an order that will never pass away.

7 Praise the LORD from the earth,
all sea monsters and ocean depths,
8 lightning and hail, snow and cloud,
stormy wind that executes his command,
9 mountains and all hills,
fruit trees and all cedars,
10 wild animals and all cattle,
creatures that crawl and flying birds,
11 kings of the earth and all peoples,
princes and all judges of the earth,
12 young men as well as young women,
old and young together.
13 Let them praise the name of the LORD,
for his name alone is exalted.
His majesty covers heaven and earth.
14 He has raised up a horn for his people,
resulting in praise to all his faithful ones,
to the Israelites, the people close to him.
Hallelujah!

Psalm 149

Praise for God's Triumph

1 Hallelujah!
Sing to the LORD a new song,
his praise in the assembly of the faithful.
2 Let Israel celebrate its Maker;
let the children of Zion rejoice in their King.
3 Let them praise his name with dancing
and make music to him with tambourine and lyre.
4 For the LORD takes pleasure in his people;
he adorns the humble with salvation.
5 Let the faithful celebrate in triumphal glory;
let them shout for joy on their beds.

6 Let the exaltation of God be in their mouths
and a double-edged sword in their hands,
7 inflicting vengeance on the nations
and punishment on the peoples,
8 binding their kings with chains
and their dignitaries with iron shackles,
9 carrying out the judgment decreed against them.
This honor is for all his faithful people.
Hallelujah!

Psalm 150

Praise the Lord

1 Hallelujah!
Praise God in his sanctuary.
Praise him in his mighty expanse.
2 Praise him for his powerful acts;
praise him for his abundant greatness.

3 Praise him with the blast of a ram's horn;
praise him with harp and lyre.
4 Praise him with tambourine and dance;
praise him with strings and flute.
5 Praise him with resounding cymbals;
praise him with clashing cymbals.

6 Let everything that breathes praise the LORD.
Hallelujah!

Daily Response

Date:

WHAT ATTRIBUTES *of* GOD STOOD OUT TO ME?

HOW DO I CONNECT *with* THE HUMAN EXPERIENCES EXPRESSED *in* TODAY'S PSALMS?

Contextual markers

Poetic devices or patterns

Words or phrases for further study

HOW HAS MY TIME READING *the* PSALMS SHAPED MY EXPERIENCE *of the* LENTEN SEASON?

HOLY *Week*

The final week of Lent is known as Holy Week, marking the last week of events in Jesus's earthy life from Palm Sunday through Resurrection Sunday. Having concluded our time in the book of Psalms, we turn our attention to the last few events of Holy Week to remember what Jesus endured to secure our right standing with God. By not shying away from the misunderstanding He endured, the accusations thrown at Him, the cross He died on, and the scars His body bore, we can more fully treasure the unimaginable miracle of the resurrection.

No matter where you are in the calendar year, we invite you to reflect on and remember these final events of Holy Week as you read. Below is a brief outline of the final days of Holy Week and the events they mark.

HOLY THURSDAY
or Maundy Thursday

Jesus shares the Last Supper with His disciples.

GOOD FRIDAY

Jesus is crucified.

HOLY SATURDAY

Jesus's body is in the tomb.

RESURRECTION SUNDAY

Jesus is raised from the dead.

The Last Supper

DAY 46  WEEK 7

Mark 14:12-72

Preparation for Passover

12 On the first day of Unleavened Bread, when they sacrifice the Passover lamb,
his disciples asked him, "Where do you want us to go and prepare the Passover so
that you may eat it?"

13 So he sent two of his disciples and told them, "Go into the city, and a man
carrying a jar of water will meet you. Follow him. 14 Wherever he enters, tell the
owner of the house, 'The Teacher says, "Where is my guest room where I may
eat the Passover with my disciples?"' 15 He will show you a large room upstairs,
furnished and ready. Make the preparations for us there." 16 So the disciples went
out, entered the city, and found it just as he had told them, and they prepared
the Passover.

Betrayal at the Passover

17 When evening came, he arrived with the Twelve. 18 While they were reclining
and eating, Jesus said, "Truly I tell you, one of you will betray me—one who is
eating with me."

19 They began to be distressed and to say to him one by one, "Surely not I?"

20 He said to them, "It is one of the Twelve—the one who is dipping bread in the
bowl with me. 21 For the Son of Man will go just as it is written about him, but
woe to that man by whom the Son of Man is betrayed! It would have been better
for him if he had not been born."

The First Lord's Supper

22 As they were eating, he took bread, blessed and broke it, gave it to them, and
said, "Take it; this is my body." 23 Then he took a cup, and after giving thanks, he
gave it to them, and they all drank from it. 24 He said to them, "This is my blood
of the covenant, which is poured out for many. 25 Truly I tell you, I will no longer
drink of the fruit of the vine until that day when I drink it new in the kingdom
of God."

26 After singing a hymn, they went out to the Mount of Olives.

Peter's Denial Predicted

27 Then Jesus said to them, "All of you will fall away, because it is written:

> I will strike the shepherd,
> and the sheep will be scattered.

28 But after I have risen, I will go ahead of you to Galilee."

29 Peter told him, "Even if everyone falls away, I will not."

30 "Truly I tell you," Jesus said to him, "today, this very night, before the rooster crows twice, you will deny me three times."

31 But he kept insisting, "If I have to die with you, I will never deny you." And they all said the same thing.

The Prayer in the Garden

32 Then they came to a place named Gethsemane, and he told his disciples, "Sit here while I pray." 33 He took Peter, James, and John with him, and he began to be deeply distressed and troubled. 34 He said to them, "I am deeply grieved to the point of death. Remain here and stay awake." 35 He went a little farther, fell to the ground, and prayed that if it were possible, the hour might pass from him. 36 And he said, "*Abba,* Father! All things are possible for you. Take this cup away from me. Nevertheless, not what I will, but what you will." 37 Then he came and found them sleeping. He said to Peter, "Simon, are you sleeping? Couldn't you stay awake one hour? 38 Stay awake and pray so that you won't enter into temptation. The spirit is willing, but the flesh is weak." 39 Once again he went away and prayed, saying the same thing. 40 And again he came and found them sleeping, because they could not keep their eyes open. They did not know what to say to him. 41 Then he came a third time and said to them, "Are you still sleeping and resting? Enough! The time has come. See, the Son of Man is betrayed into the hands of sinners. 42 Get up; let's go. See, my betrayer is near."

Judas's Betrayal of Jesus

43 While he was still speaking, Judas, one of the Twelve, suddenly arrived. With him was a mob, with swords and clubs, from the chief priests, the scribes, and the elders. 44 His betrayer had given them a signal. "The one I kiss," he said, "he's the one; arrest him and take him away under guard." 45 So when he came, immediately he went up to Jesus and said, "Rabbi!" and kissed him. 46 They took hold of him and arrested him. 47 One of those who stood by drew his sword, struck the high priest's servant, and cut off his ear.

48 Jesus said to them, "Have you come out with swords and clubs, as if I were a criminal, to capture me? 49 Every day I was among you, teaching in the temple, and you didn't arrest me. But the Scriptures must be fulfilled."

50 Then they all deserted him and ran away. 51 Now a certain young man, wearing nothing but a linen cloth, was following him. They caught hold of him, 52 but he left the linen cloth behind and ran away naked.

Jesus Faces the Sanhedrin

53 They led Jesus away to the high priest, and all the chief priests, the elders, and the scribes assembled. 54 Peter followed him at a distance, right into the high priest's courtyard. He was sitting with the servants, warming himself by the fire.

55 The chief priests and the whole Sanhedrin were looking for testimony against Jesus to put him to death, but they could not find any. 56 For many were giving false testimony against him, and the testimonies did not agree. 57 Some stood up and gave false testimony against him, stating, 58 "We heard him say, 'I will destroy this temple made with human hands, and in three days I will build another not made by hands.'" 59 Yet their testimony did not agree even on this.

60 Then the high priest stood up before them all and questioned Jesus, "Don't you have an answer to what these men are testifying against you?" 61 But he kept silent and did not answer. Again the high priest questioned him, "Are you the Messiah, the Son of the Blessed One?"

62 "I am," said Jesus, "and you will see the Son of Man seated at the right hand of Power and coming with the clouds of heaven."

63 Then the high priest tore his robes and said, "Why do we still need witnesses? 64 You have heard the blasphemy. What is your decision?" They all condemned him as deserving death.

65 Then some began to spit on him, to blindfold him, and to beat him, saying, "Prophesy!" The temple servants also took him and slapped him.

Peter Denies His Lord

66 While Peter was in the courtyard below, one of the high priest's maidservants
came. 67 When she saw Peter warming himself, she looked at him and said, "You
also were with Jesus, the man from Nazareth."

68 But he denied it: "I don't know or understand what you're talking about." Then
he went out to the entryway, and a rooster crowed.

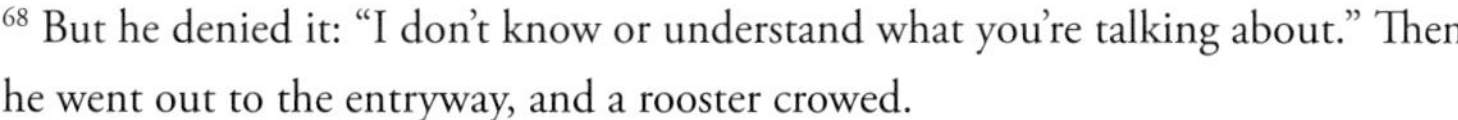

69 When the maidservant saw him again, she began to tell those standing nearby,
"This man is one of them."

70 But again he denied it. After a little while those standing there said to Peter
again, "You certainly are one of them, since you're also a Galilean."

71 Then he started to curse and swear, "I don't know this man you're talking about!"

72 Immediately a rooster crowed a second time, and Peter remembered when Jesus
had spoken the word to him, "Before the rooster crows twice, you will deny me
three times." And he broke down and wept.

Psalm 16:5

LORD, you are my portion
and my cup of blessing;
you hold my future.

John 18:28–40

Jesus Before Pilate

[28] Then they led Jesus from Caiaphas to the governor's headquarters. It was early morning. They did not enter the headquarters themselves; otherwise they would be defiled and unable to eat the Passover.

[29] So Pilate came out to them and said, "What charge do you bring against this man?"

[30] They answered him, "If this man weren't a criminal, we wouldn't have handed him over to you."

[31] Pilate told them, "You take him and judge him according to your law."

"It's not legal for us to put anyone to death," the Jews
declared. [32] They said this so that Jesus's words might be
fulfilled indicating what kind of death he was going to die.

[33] Then Pilate went back into the headquarters, summoned Jesus, and said to him, "Are you the king of the Jews?"

[34] Jesus answered, "Are you asking this on your own, or have others told you about me?"

[35] "I'm not a Jew, am I?" Pilate replied. "Your own nation and the chief priests handed you over to me. What have you done?"

[36] "My kingdom is not of this world," said Jesus. "If my kingdom were of this world, my servants would fight, so that I wouldn't be handed over to the Jews. But as it is, my kingdom is not from here."

[37] "You are a king then?" Pilate asked.

"You say that I'm a king," Jesus replied. "I was born for this, and I have come into the world for this: to testify to the truth. Everyone who is of the truth listens to my voice."

[38] "What is truth?" said Pilate.

Jesus or Barabbas

After he had said this, he went out to the Jews again and
told them, "I find no grounds for charging him. [39] You
have a custom that I release one prisoner to you at the
Passover. So, do you want me to release to you the king of
the Jews?"

40 They shouted back, "Not this man, but Barabbas!" Now Barabbas was
a revolutionary.

John 19

Jesus Flogged and Mocked

1 Then Pilate took Jesus and had him flogged. 2 The soldiers also twisted together
a crown of thorns, put it on his head, and clothed him in a purple robe. 3 And
they kept coming up to him and saying, "Hail, king of the Jews!" and were
slapping his face.

4 Pilate went outside again and said to them, "Look, I'm bringing him out to
you to let you know I find no grounds for charging him." 5 Then Jesus came out
wearing the crown of thorns and the purple robe. Pilate said to them, "Here is
the man!"

Pilate Sentences Jesus to Death

6 When the chief priests and the temple servants saw him, they shouted,
"Crucify! Crucify!"

Pilate responded, "Take him and crucify him yourselves, since I find no grounds
for charging him."

7 "We have a law," the Jews replied to him, "and according to that law he ought
to die, because he made himself the Son of God."

8 When Pilate heard this statement, he was more afraid than ever. 9 He went
back into the headquarters and asked Jesus, "Where are you from?" But Jesus
did not give him an answer. 10 So Pilate said to him, "Do you refuse to speak to
me? Don't you know that I have the authority to release you and the authority
to crucify you?"

11 "You would have no authority over me at all," Jesus answered him, "if it
hadn't been given you from above. This is why the one who handed me over to
you has the greater sin."

12 From that moment Pilate kept trying to release him. But the Jews shouted,
"If you release this man, you are not Caesar's friend. Anyone who makes himself
a king opposes Caesar!"

[13] When Pilate heard these words, he brought Jesus outside. He sat down on the judge's seat in a place called the Stone Pavement (but in Aramaic, *Gabbatha*). [14] It was the preparation day for the Passover, and it was about noon. Then he told the Jews, "Here is your king!"

[15] They shouted, "Take him away! Take him away! Crucify him!"

Pilate said to them, "Should I crucify your king?"

"We have no king but Caesar!" the chief priests answered.

[16] Then he handed him over to be crucified.

The Crucifixion

Then they took Jesus away. [17] Carrying the cross by himself, he went out to what is called Place of the Skull, which in Aramaic is called *Golgotha*. [18] There they crucified him and two others with him, one on either side, with Jesus in the middle. [19] Pilate also had a sign made and put on the cross. It said: JESUS OF NAZARETH, THE KING OF THE JEWS. [20] Many of the Jews read this sign, because the place where Jesus was crucified was near the city, and it was written in Aramaic, Latin, and Greek.
[21] So the chief priests of the Jews said to Pilate, "Don't write, 'The king of the Jews,' but that he said, 'I am the king of the Jews.'"

[22] Pilate replied, "What I have written, I have written."

[23] When the soldiers crucified Jesus, they took his clothes and divided them into four parts, a part for each soldier. They also took the tunic, which was seamless, woven in one piece from the top. [24] So they said to one another, "Let's not tear it, but cast lots for it, to see who gets it." This happened that the Scripture might be fulfilled that says: They divided my clothes among themselves, and they cast lots for my clothing. This is what the soldiers did.

Jesus's Provision for His Mother

[25] Standing by the cross of Jesus were his mother, his mother's sister, Mary the wife of Clopas, and Mary Magdalene. [26] When Jesus saw his mother and the disciple he loved standing there, he said to his mother, "Woman, here is your son." [27] Then he said to the disciple, "Here is your mother." And from that hour the disciple took her into his home.

The Finished Work of Jesus

[28] After this, when Jesus knew that everything was now finished that the Scripture might be fulfilled, he said, "I'm thirsty." [29] A jar full of sour wine was sitting there; so they fixed a sponge full of sour wine on a hyssop branch and held it up to his mouth.

NOTES

30 When Jesus had received the sour wine, he said, "It is finished." Then bowing his
head, he gave up his spirit.

Jesus's Side Pierced

31 Since it was the preparation day, the Jews did not want the bodies to remain
on the cross on the Sabbath (for that Sabbath was a special day). They requested
that Pilate have the men's legs broken and that their bodies be taken away. 32 So
the soldiers came and broke the legs of the first man and of the other one who
had been crucified with him. 33 When they came to Jesus, they did not break his
legs since they saw that he was already dead. 34 But one of the soldiers pierced
his side with a spear, and at once blood and water came out. 35 He who saw this
has testified so that you also may believe. His testimony is true, and he knows he
is telling the truth. 36 For these things happened so that the Scripture would be
fulfilled: Not one of his bones will be broken. 37 Also, another Scripture says: They
will look at the one they pierced.

Jesus's Burial

38 After this, Joseph of Arimathea, who was a disciple of Jesus—but secretly
because of his fear of the Jews—asked Pilate that he might remove Jesus's body.
Pilate gave him permission; so he came and took his body away. 39 Nicodemus
(who had previously come to him at night) also came, bringing a mixture of about
seventy-five pounds of myrrh and aloes. 40 They took Jesus's body and wrapped it
in linen cloths with the fragrant spices, according to the burial custom of the Jews.
41 There was a garden in the place where he was crucified. A new tomb was in the
garden; no one had yet been placed in it. 42 They placed Jesus there because of the
Jewish day of preparation and since the tomb was nearby.

Psalm 103:10–11

10 He has not dealt with us as our sins deserve
or repaid us according to our iniquities.

11 For as high as the heavens are above the earth,
so great is his faithful love
toward those who fear him.

Week Seven *Response*

Having concluded your time in the psalms and the first two days of our Holy Week readings, spend this Good Friday reflecting on Psalm 16:5. Talk to the Lord about whatever the psalm brings to mind. Refer back to the example on page 46 if you need to.

Psalm 16:5

Lord, you are my portion
and my cup of blessing;
you hold my future.

Holy Saturday

"TAKE GUARDS," PILATE TOLD THEM. "GO *and* MAKE IT AS SECURE AS YOU KNOW HOW."

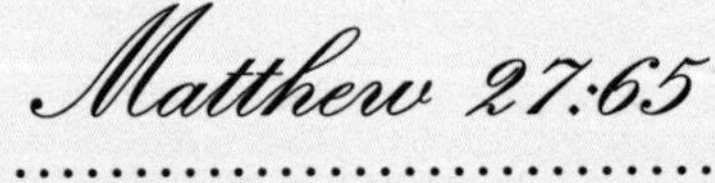

DAY 48

WEEK 7

Matthew 27:62-66

The Closely Guarded Tomb

62 The next day, which followed the preparation day, the chief
priests and the Pharisees gathered before Pilate 63 and said, "Sir,
we remember that while this deceiver was still alive he said, 'After
three days I will rise again.' 64 So give orders that the tomb be
made secure until the third day. Otherwise, his disciples may
come, steal him, and tell the people, 'He has been raised from the
dead,' and the last deception will be worse than the first."

65 "Take guards," Pilate told them. "Go and make it as secure as
you know how." 66 They went and secured the tomb by setting a
seal on the stone and placing the guards.

Luke 23:54-56

54 It was the preparation day, and the Sabbath was about to begin.
55 The women who had come with him from Galilee followed
along and observed the tomb and how his body was placed.
56 Then they returned and prepared spices and perfumes. And
they rested on the Sabbath according to the commandment.

Psalm 130:5-6

5 I wait for the LORD; I wait
and put my hope in his word.
6 I wait for the Lord
more than watchmen for the morning—
more than watchmen for the morning.

"Why are you looking for the living among the dead?" asked the men.

"He is not here, but
HE HAS RISEN!"

Luke 24:5–6

DAY 49

Easter Sunday

Week 7

Luke 24:1–12

Resurrection Morning

1 On the first day of the week, very early in the morning, they
came to the tomb, bringing the spices they had prepared. 2 They
found the stone rolled away from the tomb. 3 They went in but did
not find the body of the Lord Jesus. 4 While they were perplexed
about this, suddenly two men stood by them in dazzling clothes.
5 So the women were terrified and bowed down to the ground.

"Why are you looking for the living among the dead?" asked the
men. 6 "He is not here, but he has risen! Remember how he spoke
to you when he was still in Galilee, 7 saying, 'It is necessary that
the Son of Man be betrayed into the hands of sinful men, be
crucified, and rise on the third day'?" 8 And they remembered
his words.

9 Returning from the tomb, they reported all these things to the
Eleven and to all the rest. 10 Mary Magdalene, Joanna, Mary the
mother of James, and the other women with them were telling
the apostles these things. 11 But these words seemed like nonsense
to them, and they did not believe the women. 12 Peter, however,
got up and ran to the tomb. When he stooped to look in, he
saw only the linen cloths. So he went away, amazed at what
had happened.

Psalm 149:1–5

Praise for God's Triumph

1 Hallelujah!
Sing to the Lord a new song,
his praise in the assembly of the faithful.
2 Let Israel celebrate its Maker;
let the children of Zion rejoice in their King.
3 Let them praise his name with dancing
and make music to him with tambourine and lyre.
4 For the Lord takes pleasure in his people;
he adorns the humble with salvation.
5 Let the faithful celebrate in triumphal glory;
let them shout for joy on their beds.

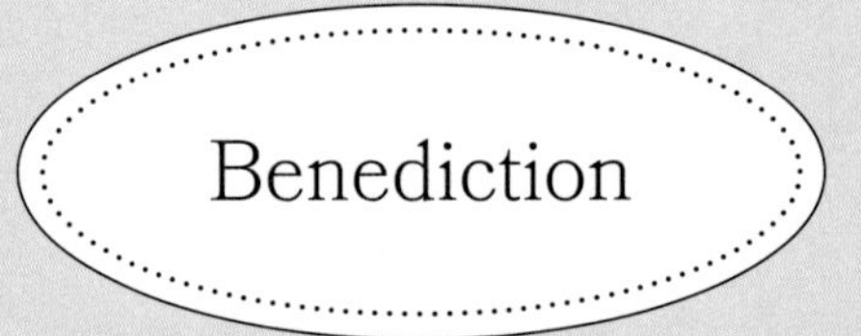
Benediction

Why did Christ come? Why was He conceived? Why was He born? Why was He crucified? Why did He rise again? Why is He now at the right hand of the Father?

THE ANSWER TO ALL THESE QUESTIONS IS,
"In order that He might make worshippers out of rebels; in order that He might restore us again to the place of worship we knew when we were first created."

A. W. Tozer

A GLOSSARY *of* TERMS *for* READING PSALMS

Terms for Understanding the Structure and Function of Psalms

Key Terminology

FOR THE CHOIR DIRECTOR:

Some psalms were entrusted to the person who was responsible for leading the community in worship.

MASKIL:

There is not a traditionally held definition for this term; some scholars believe it could be related to the idea of wisdom.

MIKTAM:

There is not a traditionally held definition for this term; some scholars have concluded that it is a term to signify that the psalm is worthy of value.

SELAH:

The exact definition is unknown; it may be a notation to signal an intentional pause.

SUPERSCRIPTION:

These are headings that the majority of psalms have containing information such as authorship, genre, liturgical directions, and situational context.

Major Categories

ENTHRONEMENT PSALMS:

These psalms focus on and celebrate the kingship and rule of God over not only Israel but all of creation. They often use phrases such as "Yahweh reigns" and rely heavily on royal imagery and metaphorical language to describe the Lord's position of power. (See Psalm 99)

HISTORICAL PSALMS:

First, this category includes psalms that reflect God's work throughout history, especially for Israel and Judah. Second, these demonstrate the psalmist's response to specific circumstances in their life, often noted in the superscription before the psalm begins. (See Psalm 105)

IMPRECATORY PSALMS:

Many of the prayers found within the book of Psalms

present requests to God to defeat, and sometimes curse, enemies. These prayers of lament focus on enemies who had committed unspeakable acts of violence against God's people and desecrated sacred places. They give voice to the desire to see evil defeated, justice prevail, and suffering cease. (See Psalm 59)

LAMENT PSALMS:

Individual and communal cries to God appear in Scripture in the form of lament psalms. These psalms not only express grief or despair but also declare faith in God's ability to save and deliver. (See Psalm 42)

PRAISE PSALMS:

While the entirety of the Psalter demonstrates praise, specific psalms praise God for His character and actions or praise Him in light of the individual circumstances where the psalmists experienced Him. More specifically, some praise psalms are distinguished by opening with the Hebrew word *halal* (meaning "hallelujah"). (See Psalm 146)

WISDOM PSALMS:

Similar to Job, Proverbs, and Ecclesiastes, the wisdom psalms encourage personal contemplation on life and faith. These psalms encourage the reader to meditate on and respond to God's Word. They are reflections more than prayers, guiding us to consider our lives and our struggles in light of what is true. (See Psalm 1)

Poetic Devices

ACROSTIC:

A poem where the first letter of each line forms a word, phrase, or pattern in the original language (See Psalm 119)

APOSTROPHE:

An address to an absent subject as though they were present (See Psalm 148)

CHIASM:

A form of parallelism that organizes a series of ideas, narratives, phrases, or sections in a mirrored pattern, presenting thoughts and then repeating them in reverse order (See Psalm 90)

HYPERBOLE:

An intentional exaggeration for increased effect (See Psalm 42:3)

METAPHOR:

A figure of speech that states one subject is another for comparison (See Psalm 23:1)

PARALLELISM:

The repetition of similar words, phrases, or ideas in multiple lines; sometimes an idea is repeated in new terms, expounded on more specifically, or countered to add emphasis to an idea (See Psalm 27:1)

Continued

A GLOSSARY *of* TERMS *for* READING PSALMS

PERSONIFICATION:

Assigning human attributes to nonhuman things, events, or God (sometimes called anthropomorphism) (See Psalm 43:3)

SIMILE:

A comparison between two ideas using the words *like* or *as* (See Psalm 1:3)

Terms Found Within Psalms

Key Places

BASHAN:

A region in the upper Transjordan located east of the Sea of Galilee; control of the territory often changed but was at one point conquered by the Israelites; known for its fertile land

JERUSALEM:

The primary city of biblical Israel and later the southern kingdom of Judah

LEBANON:

A mountain region located north of Israel; the cedars that grew in its forest were highly valued and used for significant building projects noted in the Old Testament

SHEOL:

A term that is used to describe death itself or the dwelling place of the dead; often described as a place of punishment; only the Lord can deliver people from here

ZION:

A term often used for the whole of Jerusalem or the people of Israel; also signifies the dwelling of God's presence

Key People

ASAPH:

Worship leader and songwriter during the time of David

DAVID:

The anointed shepherd who became Israel's second king; promised forefather of the Messiah

HEMAN AND ETHAN THE EZRAHITES:

Brothers known for their wisdom; temple singers during the time of David; relatives of Asaph

MOSES:

An influential leader from the fifteenth century BC who led the people of Israel out of Egypt to the edge of the promised land and received the Old Testament law from God at Mount Sinai; authorship of the first five books of the Bible has been traditionally attributed to him

SOLOMON:

King David's son and Israel's third king who was known for his God-given wisdom

SONS OF KORAH:

Worship leaders during the time of King Jehoshaphat

Common Words and Phrases

FAITHFUL LOVE:

From the Hebrew word *hesed* which signifies God's unfailing, covenantal love

HALLELUJAH:

A liturgical interjection signifying boastful praise

LORD:

Modern English translations of the Bible often use small capital letters (LORD or GOD) for *Yahweh;* distinct from other names of God because it is self-revealed; the intimate, covenantal, relational name of God

PRECEPTS:

The commands found in God's law

REFUGE:

A place of shelter or relief from danger or distress

RIGHT HAND:

Can refer to someone's literal right hand; represents authority and power; to be at someone's right hand is to be in a position of honor; God is described as performing mighty acts of blessing with His right hand

RIGHTEOUS/ RIGHTEOUSNESS:

An adherence to God's just, upright standard

STRONGHOLD:

A secure place of safety and protection

Tips for Memorizing Scripture

At She Reads Truth, we believe Scripture memorization is an important discipline in your walk with God. Committing God's Word to memory means we carry it with us and we can minister to others wherever we go. As you approach the Weekly Truth verses in this book, try these memorization tips to see which techniques work best for you!

STUDY IT

Study the passage in its biblical context, and ask yourself a few questions before you begin to memorize it: What does this passage say? What does it mean? How would I say this in my own words? What does it teach me about God? Understanding what the passage means helps you know why it is important to carry it with you wherever you go.

Break the passage into smaller sections, memorizing a phrase at a time.

PRAY IT

Use the passage you are memorizing as a prompt for prayer.

WRITE IT

Dedicate a notebook to Scripture memorization, and write the passage over and over again.

Diagram the passage after you write it out. Place a square around the verbs, underline the nouns, and circle any adjectives or adverbs. Say the passage aloud several times, emphasizing the verbs as you repeat it. Then do the same thing again with the nouns, then the adjectives and adverbs.

Write out the first letter of each word in the passage somewhere you can reference it throughout the week as you work on your memorization.

Use a whiteboard to write out the passage. Erase a few words at a time as you continue to repeat it aloud. Keep erasing parts of the passage until you have it all committed to memory.

CREATE

If you can, make up a tune for the passage to sing as you go about your day, or try singing it to the tune of a favorite song.

Sketch the passage, visualizing what each phrase would look like in the form of a picture. Or try using calligraphy or altering the style of your handwriting as you write it out.

Use hand signals or signs to come up with associations for each word or phrase, and repeat the movements as you practice.

SAY IT

Repeat the passage out loud to yourself as you are going through the rhythm of your day—getting ready, pouring your coffee, waiting in traffic, or making dinner.

Listen to the passage read aloud to you.

Record a voice memo on your phone, and listen to it throughout the day, or play it on an audio Bible.

SHARE IT

Memorize the passage with a friend, family member, or mentor. Spontaneously challenge each other to recite the passage, or pick a time to review your passage and practice saying it from memory together.

Send the passage as an encouraging text to a friend, testing yourself as you type to see how much you have memorized so far.

KEEP AT IT!

Set reminders on your phone to prompt you to practice your passage.

Purchase a She Reads Truth Scripture Card Set, or keep a stack of note cards with Scripture you are memorizing by your bed. Practice reciting what you've memorized previously before you go to sleep, ending with the passages you are currently learning. If you wake up in the middle of the night, review them again instead of grabbing your phone. Read them out loud before you get out of bed in the morning.

CSB BOOK ABBREVIATIONS

OLD TESTAMENT

GN Genesis
EX Exodus
LV Leviticus
NM Numbers
DT Deuteronomy
JOS Joshua
JDG Judges
RU Ruth
1SM 1 Samuel
2SM 2 Samuel
1KG 1 Kings
2KG 2 Kings
1CH 1 Chronicles
2CH 2 Chronicles
EZR Ezra
NEH Nehemiah
EST Esther
JB Job
PS Psalms
PR Proverbs
EC Ecclesiastes
SG Song of Solomon
IS Isaiah
JR Jeremiah
LM Lamentations
EZK Ezekiel
DN Daniel
HS Hosea
JL Joel
AM Amos
OB Obadiah
JNH Jonah
MC Micah
NAH Nahum
HAB Habakkuk
ZPH Zephaniah
HG Haggai
ZCH Zechariah
MAL Malachi

NEW TESTAMENT

MT Matthew
MK Mark
LK Luke
JN John
AC Acts
RM Romans
1CO 1 Corinthians
2CO 2 Corinthians
GL Galatians
EPH Ephesians
PHP Philippians
COL Colossians
1TH 1 Thessalonians
2TH 2 Thessalonians
1TM 1 Timothy
2TM 2 Timothy
TI Titus
PHM Philemon
HEB Hebrews
JMS James
1PT 1 Peter
2PT 2 Peter
1JN 1 John
2JN 2 John
3JN 3 John
JD Jude
RV Revelation

BIBLIOGRAPHY

Bilkes, Gerald M. "Selah." In *Eerdmans Dictionary of the Bible,* edited by David Noel Freedman, Allen C. Myers, and Astrid B. Beck. Eerdmans, 2000.

Breslich, A. L. "Hallelujah." In *The International Standard Bible Encyclopaedia,* Vol. 1–5, edited by James Orr, John L. Nuelsen, Edgar Y. Mullins, and Morris O. Evans. The Howard-Severance Company, 1915.

Brisco, Thomas V. "Lebanon." In *Eerdmans Dictionary of the Bible,* edited by David Noel Freedman, Allen C. Myers, and Astrid B. Beck. Eerdmans, 2000.

Dorman, David A. "Refuge." In *Eerdmans Dictionary of the Bible,* edited by David Noel Freedman, Allen C. Myers, and Astrid B. Beck. Eerdmans, 2000.

Duvall, J. Scott, and J. Daniel Hays. *Grasping God's Word.* 4th ed. Zondervan, 2020.

"Hallel." In *Holman Illustrated Bible Dictionary,* edited by Chad Brand, Eric Alan Mitchell, Steve Bond, E. Ray Clendenen, and Trent C. Butler. Holman Bible Publishers, 2003.

Longman III, Tremper. *Psalms: An Introduction and Commentary,* Vol. 15–16. Tyndale Old Testament Commentaries. Inter-Varsity Press, 2014.

Neal, D. A. "Sheol." In *The Lexham Bible Dictionary,* edited by John D. Barry, David Bomar, and Derek R. Brown, et al. Lexham Press, 2016.

Park, Aaron W. "Zion." In *Eerdmans Dictionary of the Bible,* edited by David Noel Freedman, Allen C. Myers, and Astrid B. Beck. Eerdmans, 2000.

Shepherd, C. E. "Jerusalem." In *The Lexham Bible Dictionary,* edited by John D. Barry, David Bomar, and Derek R. Brown, et al. Lexham Press, 2016.

Thomas, Robert L. *New American Standard Hebrew-Aramaic and Greek Dictionaries:* Updated ed. Foundation Publications, Inc., 1998.

Tozer, A. W. *Whatever Happened to Worship?* Revised ed. Wingspread Publishers, 2012.

Tucker, Jr., W. Dennis. "Choirmaster." In *Eerdmans Dictionary of the Bible,* edited by David Noel Freedman, Allen C. Myers, and Astrid B. Beck. Eerdmans, 2000.

West, Jim "Sheol." In *Eerdmans Dictionary of the Bible,* edited by David Noel Freedman, Allen C. Myers, and Astrid B. Beck. Eerdmans, 2000.

Whitney, Donald S. *Praying the Bible.* Crossway, 2015.

Williams, Tyler F. "Miktam." In *Eerdmans Dictionary of the Bible,* edited by David Noel Freedman, Allen C. Myers, and Astrid B. Beck. Eerdmans, 2000.

Williams, Tyler F. "Superscription." In *Eerdmans Dictionary of the Bible,* edited by David Noel Freedman, Allen C. Myers, and Astrid B. Beck. Eerdmans, 2000.

Wolfe, Gregory A. "Right Hand." In *Eerdmans Dictionary of the Bible,* edited by David Noel Freedman, Allen C. Myers, and Astrid B. Beck. Eerdmans, 2000.

Younker, Randall W. "Bashan." In *Eerdmans Dictionary of the Bible,* edited by David Noel Freedman, Allen C. Myers, and Astrid B. Beck. Eerdmans, 2000.

You just spent 49 days in the Word of God!

MY FAVORITE DAY OF THIS READING PLAN:

ONE THING I LEARNED ABOUT GOD:

WHAT WAS GOD DOING IN MY LIFE DURING THIS STUDY?

HOW DID I FIND DELIGHT IN GOD'S WORD?

WHAT DID I LEARN THAT I WANT TO SHARE WITH SOMEONE ELSE?

A SPECIFIC PASSAGE OR VERSE THAT ENCOURAGED ME:

A SPECIFIC PASSAGE OR VERSE THAT CHALLENGED AND CONVICTED ME: